THE BEATITUDES
and
THE LORD'S PRAYER
for everyman

William Barclay

THE BEATITUDES
and
THE LORD'S PRAYER
for everyman

1817

HARPER & ROW, PUBLISHERS

New York, Evanston, San Francisco, London

*the text of this book is printed
on 100% recycled paper*

The Beatitudes and the Lord's Prayer for Everyman was published
in England in separate volumes entitled *The Plain Man Looks at
the Beatitudes* and *The Plain Man Looks at the Lord's Prayer*.

FIRST HARPER & ROW paperback edition published in 1975.

LIBRARY OF CONGRESS CATALOG CARD NUMBER: 75-9309

ISBN: 0-06-060393-3

80   12 11 10 9 8 7 6 5 4 3

CONTENTS

THE BEATITUDES

THE LORD'S PRAYER

THE BEATITUDES

*To the students of Trinity College,
past and present, who have already
heard what is in this book*

AUTHOR'S NOTE

The chapters of this book have a double origin. In the first place, they represent the substance of lectures given over the years to my students in Trinity College, Glasgow.

In lecturing over the years a man uses many sources, and in the end he so integrates material into his own lectures that he forgets what is his own and what he has borrowed from other sources. I hope that if I have, in these chapters, failed to acknowledge any borrowings, the people from whom I have borrowed will understand and forgive.

In the second place, these chapters originally appeared as a series of articles in the *Preachers' Quarterly*. I have to thank the editor of that magazine for, in the first place, allowing me the courtesy of his columns and, in the second place, allowing me to issue these chapters as a book.

The author and publisher thank the following for kind permission to quote from the works mentioned: The Society of Authors as the literary representative of the Estate of the late A. E. Housman, and Messrs Jonathan Cape Ltd., publishers of A. E. Housman's *Collected Poems*; Hodder & Stoughton Ltd., *The Best of Studdert Kennedy*; G. Bell & Sons Ltd., Aristophanes' *Plutus* translated by B. B. Rogers.

THE ESSENCE OF THE ESSENCE

For most people the Sermon on the Mount is the essence of the Christian faith and life; and equally for most people the Beatitudes are the essence of the Sermon on the Mount. It is therefore not too much to say that the Beatitudes are the essence of the essence of the Christian way of life.

In this case the findings of the New Testament scholarship have confirmed that which the ordinary person instinctively feels. The detailed study of the Sermon on the Mount confirms the conviction that it is indeed the central document of the Christian faith. Three times in his introduction to it Matthew makes that clear (Matthew 5.1,2):

> And seeing the multitudes Jesus went up into a mountain; and, when he was set, his disciples came unto him; and he opened his mouth and taught them.

i. *When he was set* means *when he had sat down*. Often a Jewish Rabbi would talk to his disciples when he was walking along the road with them, or when he was strolling in some city square or colonnade; but when he was teaching, as we might put it, officially, he always sat to do so. This was the Jewish attitude of official teaching. In the Synagogue the preacher sat to deliver the sermon. We still talk of a professor's *chair,* which was the chair in which he sat to deliver his lectures to his students. When the Pope makes an official announcement he speaks *ex cathedra,* seated in his papal throne. From this introduction Matthew means us to see that what follows is no chance teaching given in the by-going; it is no pleasant discourse given in the passing; it is the official teaching of Jesus. It is Jesus telling his disciples the very essence of what he came to say.

ii. The phrase *he opened his mouth* is more than an elaborate or poetical way of saying *he said.* It has certain overtones and implications.

a. It is regularly used to introduce any weighty, grave and important utterance. It is the phrase of the great occasion. It is used, for instance, of the utterance of an oracle, which the hearer will neglect at his peril. In the New Testament itself this phrase is used on two very significant occasions. It is used of Philip expounding the meaning of scripture to the Ethiopian eunuch (Acts 8.35). Philip was giving the Ethiopian an authoritative exposition of the message of scripture regarding Jesus. It is used of Peter, when, after the conversion of the Roman centurion Cornelius, he expounded the epoch-making discovery that the gospel was for the Gentiles also (Acts 10.34). This phrase is regularly the preface to some pronouncement of the greatest weight and importance, and it is the warning that there is something to follow which must not be lightly disregarded.

b. It is used of an utterance of calculated courage. A phrase very closely kin to it is used by the great Greek orator Isocrates in the last speech he ever made, his final witness and testimonial to the glory of Athens. On that occasion he says that he is moved to use the greatest freedom of speech, whatever the consequence may be, and to *remove the curb from his tongue* (*Panathenaicus* 96). It is used of a speaker who will shrink from saying nothing that ought to be said, and who will speak, fearless of anything that men may do to him.

c. It is used of an utterance in which there are no reservations, in which nothing is kept back, and in which the whole truth is told and the whole heart opened. In Aeschylus' *Prometheus Vinctus,* when Io asks for information about the future, Prometheus answers: "I will tell thee plainly all that thou art fain to know . . . even as it is right *to open the lips* to friends." The whole atmosphere of the phrase is the opening of the mind and the heart in such a way that nothing is kept back.

By using this phrase of Jesus Matthew warns us that there is to follow an utterance of the greatest weight and importance, an utterance in which no cautious and prudential motives of safety will keep the speaker from telling the truth, an utterance in which mind and heart are opened and in which nothing is kept back.

iii. Matthew says that Jesus *taught* his disciples. In Greek there are two past tenses of the verb. There is the *aorist* which describes one completed action in past time. There is the *imperfect* which describes repeated and habitual action in past time. "He shut the door behind him," would be expressed by an aorist tense; "it was his habit always to shut doors behind him," would be expressed by an imperfect tense. The tense in Matthew's introduction is the imperfect tense. Therefore in what follows we are to see, not simply a statement made by Jesus on one occasion, but the substance of all that he habitually and repeatedly taught his disciples. We are not to see here only one sermon; we are to see the summary of the teaching which Jesus continually and consistently gave to his disciples. It is therefore nothing more than the actual fact to say that the Sermon on the Mount is the essence of the teaching of Jesus.

All Matthew's phrases converge to show how essential to the teaching of Jesus the material which is to follow is. It therefore follows that the study of the Beatitudes is one of the most important studies to which the Christian, or the man who wishes to find out the meaning of Christianity, can devote himself.

THE DIVINE BLISS

The Authorised Version prints the Beatitudes as statements; but in each case it prints the *are* in italic print, which is the conventional sign that there is no corresponding word in the Greek text. In the Greek there is no verb in any of the Beatitudes, which means that the Beatitudes are not statements, but exclamations. They reproduce in Greek a form of expression which is very common in Hebrew, especially in the Psalms. Hebrew has an exclamatory word *ashere,* which means: " O the bliss of . . ." So the Psalmist says: " O the bliss of the man who walks not in the counsel of the ungodly . . . but whose delight is in the law of the Lord " (Psalm 1. 1). " O the bliss of the man to whom the Lord does not impute iniquity, and in whose spirit there is no guile " (Psalm 32. 2). " O the bliss of the man whom thou chastenest, O Lord, and teachest him out of thy law " (Psalm 94. 12). This is the form of expression which each of the Beatitudes represents; each of them is an exclamation beginning: " O the bliss of . . . !" That is to say that the Beatitudes are not promises of future happiness; they are congratulations on present bliss. They are not statements and prophecies of what is one day going to happen to the Christian in some other world; they are affirmations of the bliss into which

the Christian can enter even here and now. That is not
to say that this bliss will not reach its perfection and its
completion, when some day the Christian enters into the
nearer presence of his Lord; but it is to say that even
here and now the foretaste and the experience of that
bliss is meant to be part of the Christian life.

And what is that bliss? The word which is translated
blessed is the word *makarios,* which in its older form in
Greek was *makar.* The characteristic of that word is that
properly it describes a bliss which belongs only to the
gods. Although the word lost something of its greatness
and came to be used in a wider and a looser sense, the
fact remains that in Greek thought only the gods were
truly *hoi makarioi,* the Blessed Ones. In the New
Testament itself God himself is twice described by this
word. In the pastoral Epistles we read of the glorious
gospel of the *blessed* God, and God is called the *blessed*
and only Potentate, the King of kings and Lord of
lords (I Timothy 1. 11; 6. 15). Two further uses of this
word will make its meaning clearer yet. It is used of the
Blessed Isles, the place of perfect happiness to which the
blessed go, the place where pain and sorrow and hunger
and all distress are gone, and where there is a serenity
and a joy which nothing can touch (Pindar, *Olympians*
2. 70). Again, Herodotus uses this word to describe an
oasis in the desert (Herodotus 3. 26). All around there
is the desert with its sand and its thirst and its agony
of body and of spirit; in the oasis there is shade and
shelter, and peace for the weary traveller. F. W.
Boreham quotes a tradition that Cyprus was in ancient
times called *He Makaria,* the Blessed Isle, because the

climate was so perfect, the soil so fertile, and the natural resources so complete, that he who dwelt in Cyprus never needed to go beyond it to find his perfect happiness and all his needs supplied.

Here we have our answer. The promised bliss is nothing less than the blessedness of God. Through Jesus Christ the Christian comes to share in the very life of God. The bliss of the Beatitudes is another expression of what John calls Eternal Life. Eternal life is *zoe aionios;* in Greek there is only one person in the universe to whom the word *aionios* may properly be applied, and that person is God. Eternal life is nothing less than the life of God, and it is a share in that life that Jesus Christ offers to men.

If that is so, it means that the Christian bliss is independent of outward circumstances; like the island of Cyprus, it has within itself all it needs for perfect happiness. It is independent of all the chances and the changes of life. That, indeed, is why happiness is not a good name for it. Happiness has in it the root *hap,* which means *chance;* and happiness is something which is dependent on the chances and alterations of this life; but the Christian bliss is the bliss of the life of God, and is, therefore, the joy that no man can take from us.

If this Christian bliss is the bliss of the blessedness of God, we will not be surprised to find that it completely reverses the world's standards. O the bliss of the poor! O the bliss of the sorrowful! O the bliss of the hungry and thirsty! O the bliss of the persecuted! These are startling contradictions of the world's standards; these are sayings which no man could hear for the first time without a shock of amazement. Deissmann said of the Beatitudes: "They are not quiet stars, but flashes of lightning, followed by a thunder of surprise and amazement." But when we look at the Beatitudes carefully, we see that they are very closely interwoven into a threefold bliss.

There is the bliss which comes when a man recognises his deepest need, and discovers where that need can be supplied. There can be three periods in any life. There can be the period when a man lives placidly and in a kind of drab mediocrity, because he knows nothing better. There can be a period of restless dissatisfaction and even of mental agony, when something makes him realize that there is an unidentified something missing in his life. And there can be the period into which there enters a new joy and a new depth into life, because a man has found that wherein his newly discovered need can be supplied. So there is bliss for the man who discovers his own poverty, for the man who becomes sorrowfully aware of his own sin, and for the man who hungers and thirsts for a righteousness which he knows is not in him.

There is the bliss of living the Christian life. There is the bliss which comes in living in mercy, in meekness, in purity of heart, and in the making of peace. These were the qualities of Jesus Christ himself, and he who follows in the steps of Jesus Christ knows the joy of the Christian life.

There is the bliss of suffering for Jesus Christ. Long ago Plato said that the good man will always choose to suffer wrong rather than to do wrong. Herein is the bliss of loyalty, and there is the deepest of all satisfactions in loyalty, even when loyalty costs all that a man has to give.

On the face of it, it might look as if the Beatitudes looked for bliss all in the wrong places; but when we think again we can see that the way of the Beatitudes is the only way to bliss.

THE BLISS OF THE DESTITUTE

Blessed are the poor in spirit, for theirs is the kingdom of heaven (MATTHEW 5. 3).

Jesus could hardly have produced a more startling beginning to his Beatitudes. And Luke has it even more uncompromisingly: Blessed be ye poor, for yours is the kingdom of God (Luke 6. 20). There are very few people who would agree that poverty is a blessing, or that there is any bliss to be found in destitution. Dr. Johnson lays it down: "Resolve not to be poor . . . Poverty is a great enemy to human happiness; it certainly destroys liberty, and it makes some virtues impracticable, and others extremely difficult." Most people would speak of the curse of poverty rather than of the blessing of poverty.

The more closely we examine this saying, the more startling it becomes. The word which is used in the Greek for *poor* is *ptochos,* which is the adjective to describe, not one who is simply poor, but one who is completely destitute. The Greeks connected *ptochos* with the verb *ptossein* which means *to crouch* or *to cower,* and which Homer uses to describe the *cringing* of a suppliant beggar (Homer, *Odyssey* 17. 227). Aeschylus shows us Cassandra stripping off the insignia of a prophetess, and deciding to become a vagrant, *begging gipsy* (Aeschylus, *Agamemnon* 1274). When the wretched Oedipus had lost his kingdom, and everything with it, Sophocles describes him as reduced to *penury,* a man in exile and a beggar (Sophocles, *Oedipus Coloneus* 444. 751). Herodotus uses the word *ptochos* to describe a man, who was well-born and who had once been rich, and who is reduced to begging scraps of food from the soldiers to keep body and soul together (Herodotus 3. 14). In the Code of Justinian the corresponding noun *ptocheia* means *poor relief.* For the man who is *ptochos* there is nothing left in this world but the poor-house.

But Greek has two words for *poor.* The second is the word *penes,* which describes the man who has nothing superfluous, the man who has to work for his living, the man who has to satisfy his needs with the work of his hands. Such a man is *autodiakonos,* under the necessity of serving himself. Socrates frequently described himself as *penes,* because he had given so much time to the gods that he had no time to build up a lucrative career for himself (Plato, *Apology* 23 C). But Socrates was in no danger of imminent starvation, however frugal his life might be. But the word *ptochos,* the other word for *poor,* describes, not the man who has nothing superfluous, but the man who has nothing at all. In the *Plutus* of Aristophanes *Penia,* Poverty, is one of the characters, and she herself draws a distinction between the man who is *penes* and the man who is *ptochos,* between the man who is poor and frugal and the man who is destitute and a beggar (Aristophanes, *Plutus* 550-554; Rogers' translation) :

But the life I allot to my people is not, nor shall be
so full of distresses.

'Tis a beggar (*ptochos*) alone who has naught of his
own, nor even an obol (i.e. a penny piece)
possesses.

My poor man (*penes*) 'tis true, has to scrape and to
screw, and his work he must never be slack in;

There'll be no superfluity found in his cot; but then
there will nothing be lacking.

In this Beatitude Tertullian alters the translation of
the Vulgate (*Against Marcion* 4. 14). The Vulgate
has: "Blessed are the *pauperes,* that is, the *poor.*"
Tertullian alters it to: "Blessed are the *mendici,* that
is, the beggars."

In the eyes of the Greek there was something wretched
and pitiable and even shameful in this word *ptochos.*
In his legislation for the ideal state Plato banishes the
ptochos from the community. "There shall be no
beggar (*ptochos*) in our state; and, if anyone attempts
to beg . . . he shall be driven across the border by the
country stewards, to the end that the land may be wholly
purged by such a creature" (Plato, *Laws* 936 C). In
the Gospels themselves the word *ptochos* describes the
wretched Lazarus who was daily dumped to beg at the
gate of the rich man (Luke 16. 20, 21); the widow whose
total possessions amounted to two mites, half a farthing
(Mark 12. 42, 43); the vagrants who were to be brought
in from the highways and the hedges to be the
unexpected guests at the banquet of the king (Luke
14. 21). It is by the word *ptochos* that James describes

the poor man who is contemptuously pushed aside to give the rich man the place of prominence and honour (James 2. 2, 3).

Milligan rightly remarks that the word *ptochos* was always used in a bad sense, until it was ennobled by the gospel. It would be difficult to find a word which to pagan ears had more of humiliation in it than the word *ptochos*.

But this is only one side of the picture. Jesus did not speak in Greek; he spoke in Aramaic; and his thought and language had their source and origin in the Old Testament. *Ptochos* represents the Old Testament word *ani*, which is generally translated *poor*, but which had acquired a special and distinctive meaning in the devotional literature of the Old Testament. The word *ani* underwent a four stage development of meaning in Hebrew. i. Originally it meant *poor* in the literal sense of the term. ii. A poor man is a man who has no power, no prestige, no influence to defend himself against the insults and the assaults of the world. iii. Such a man will be downtrodden and oppressed, and pushed to the wall in the competitive society of this world. iv. But such a man, in spite of everything, may retain his integrity and his devotion, and may be convinced that it is better to be humiliated with God than it is to be prosperous with the world. Hence the word *ani* came finally to describe the poor, humble, faithful man, who has no help on earth, and who in perfect trust has wholly committed himself to God.

In this sense the word *ani* becomes characteristic of the Psalms. "This poor man (*ani*) cried, and the Lord heard him, and saved him out of his troubles " (Psalm 34. 6; cp. Psalm 35. 10; 40. 17; 72. 2).

So, then, when we bring together the Greek and the Hebrew background of this word *poor,* we see that it describes the man who has fully realized his own inadequacy, his own worthlessness, and his own destitution, and who has put his whole trust in God. It describes the man who has realized that by himself life is impossible but that with God all things are possible; the man who has become so dependent on God that he has become independent of everything else in the universe.

This Beatitude has in it a whole attitude to life. It has in it three basic truths about life.

i. It means that the way to power lies through the realization of helplessness; that the way to victory lies through the admission of defeat; that the way to goodness lies through the confession and the acknowledgment of sin. Herein is an essential truth which runs through all life. If a man is ill, the first necessity is that he should admit and recognise that he is ill, and that then he should seek for a cure in the right place. The way to knowledge begins with the admission of ignorance. The one man who can never learn is the man who thinks that he knows everything already. Plato said: " He is the wisest man who knows himself to be very ill-qualified for the attainment of wisdom." Quintilian, the Roman master of oratory, said of certain of his students: " They would doubtless have become excellent scholars, if they had not been so fully persuaded of their own scholarship." This Beatitude affirms the basic fact that the first necessity towards the attainment of fulness of life is a sense of need.

ii. The second thing which this Beatitude does is to make a complete revaluation of what constitutes wealth. It lays it down that true wealth can never consist in the possession of things. The man who has nothing but money with which to meet life is a poverty-stricken man. The essential characteristic of material things is their insecurity. There is none of them which cannot be lost, often all unexpectedly and without warning. It was this fact of life which produced Solon's grim saying. Solon was visiting Croesus of Sardis. He saw Croesus in all his wealth and absolutely confident in the future. " Call no man happy," said Solon grimly, " until he is dead." This Beatitude lays it down that the man who has put his trust in that which his own skill or ingenuity can acquire has put his trust in the wrong place, and that before life ends he will make the tragic discovery that he has done so.

iii. The third thing which this Beatitude teaches is that the way to independence lies through dependence, and the way to freedom lies through surrender. If ever a man is to be independent of the chances and the changes of life, that independence must come from his complete dependence on God. If ever a man is to know true freedom, that freedom must come through complete surrender to God.

This Beatitude lays down that the way to the bliss which the world can neither give nor take away lies through the recognition of our own need, and the conviction that that need can be met, when we commit to God in perfect trust.

Each of the Beatitudes contains, not only an affirmation, but also a promise. " Blessed are the poor in spirit ", says this Beatitude, and then it goes on to promise, " for theirs is the kindom of heaven." What, then, is the meaning of this promise which is made to the poor in spirit? What is the kingdom of heaven?

We must first note that the two phrases *the kingdom of heaven* and *the kingdom of God* mean exactly the same thing. In the Gospels Matthew almost invariably speaks of *the kingdom of heaven,* and Mark and Luke almost invariably speak of *the kingdom of God.* The reason for the difference in practice lies in this. Such was the reverence of a strict and orthodox Jew that he would never, if he could avoid it, take the name of God upon his lips. He always, if possible, used some periphrasis to avoid actually uttering the name of God. It is very natural that by far the commonest periphrasis for God is in fact heaven. Matthew is the most Jewish of the Gospel writers; Mark was not so strictly Jewish; and Luke was a Gentile, who was not bound at all by the Jewish conventions and customs. So it comes about that Matthew with his strong orthodox Jewish background prefers to speak of *the kingdom of heaven,* while Mark and Luke, being less affected by Jewish tradition, have no hesitation in speaking of *the kingdom of God.*

If we wish to define the kingdom of God, we may best find the basis of our definition in the Lord's Prayer. The outstanding characteristic of Jewish literary style is parallelism. The Jew tended to say everything twice;

and the second form of expression is a repetition, an amplification, or an explanation of the first. Almost any verse of the Psalms will demonstrate this characteristic. Almost all the verses of the Psalms have a division in the middle, and the second half of the verse repeats or amplifies the first half.

> God is our refuge and our strength,
> A very present help in trouble (Psalm 46. 1).

> The Lord of hosts is with us;
> The God of Jacob is our refuge (Psalm 46. 7).

> He maketh me to lie down in green pastures;
> He leadeth me beside the still waters (Psalm 23. 2).

In the Lord's Prayer two phrases occur side by side (Matthew 6. 10):

> Thy kingdom come,
> Thy will be done in earth as it is in heaven.

Let us, then, apply the principle of parallelism to these two phrases, and let us assume that the second explains and interprets the first. We then arrive at the definition: The kingdom of God is a society upon earth in which God's will is as perfectly done as it is in heaven.

Quite clearly this personalises the kingdom of God, for such a society cannot begin to exist until each individual man and woman perfectly accepts the will of God. That is to say, whenever anyone fully accepts the will of God, that person is within the kingdom of God. No man can be a citizen of any country, unless he is willing to accept the laws of that country; citizenship and obedience to a country's laws go hand in hand. Exactly in the same way, no man can be a citizen of the kingdom of God, until he fully accepts the laws of God. To be a citizen of the kingdom of God, to be in the kingdom of God, to possess the kingdom of God, all mean perfectly to accept the will of God.

If that be so, this Beatitude is saying: O the bliss of the man who has realized his own utter helplessness and his own utter inadequacy, and who has put his whole trust in God; for then he will humbly accept the will of God, and in so doing he will become a citizen of the kingdom of God. And that is precisely the origin of the bliss, for in doing his will is our peace.

THE BLISS OF THE BROKEN-HEARTED

Blessed are they that mourn, for they shall be comforted
(MATTHEW 5. 4).

Of all the paradoxes of the Beatitudes surely this is the
most violent. It is an astonishing thing to speak of the
joy of sorrow, of the gladness of grief, and of the bliss of
the broken-hearted. The word which the Authorised
Version translates *mourn* (*penthein*) is one of the
strongest words for mourning in the Greek language.
It is used for mourning for the dead. Very often it is
associated with the word *klaiein*, which means *to weep*,
and it signifies the sorrow which issues in tears.

From the very word which is used to describe this
mourning two things are immediately clear. It is the
sorrow which pierces the heart; it is no gentle, sentimental, twilight sadness, in which a man can languish
and luxuriate; it is a sorrow which is poignant, piercing
and intense. It is the sorrow which is visible; it is the
sorrow which can be seen in a man's bearing, a man's
face, and a man's tears. It is the sorrow which a man is
bound to show to the world and to show to God, because
he cannot help doing so. What, then, did Jesus mean,
when He spoke of the bliss of the broken-hearted?

i. It may well be that, at least to some extent, this Beatitude is meant to be taken quite literally. There is no doubt that sorrow has a value of its own, and that it has a place in life which nothing else can take. There is always something missing in life, until sorrow has entered into life. There is an Arab proverb which says: " All sunshine makes a desert." It is told that once Elgar, the great musician, was listening to a young girl singing. She had a beautiful voice and a well-nigh faultless technique, but she just missed greatness. " She will be great," said Elgar, " when something happens to break her heart." There are things which only sorrow can teach.

It might well be said that sorrow is the source of the great discoveries in life. It is in sorrow that a man discovers the things which matter, and the things which do not matter. It is in sorrow that a man discovers the meaning of friendship and the meaning of love. It is in sorrow that a man discovers whether his faith is a merely superficial ornament of life or the essential foundation on which his whole life depends. It is in sorrow that a man discovers God. " When you come to the bottom," said Neville Talbot, " you find God."

There is a deep sense in which it is literally true that sorrow has its own unique blessedness to give.

ii. Luke repeats this Beatitude in a slightly different form: " Blessed are ye that weep now, for ye shall laugh " (Luke 6. 21). It would seem that Luke was thinking in terms of the necessary struggle of the Christian life, and that he meant that, if a man accepts the cross which is at the heart of the Christian life, then quite certainly he will win the crown.

Luke had firmly grasped the truth that in this life and from this life a man gets what he chooses. If he chooses to live as if nothing mattered beyond this world, then he gets all that this world has to offer. But, if he chooses to live in the conviction that there is something far more important beyond this world, then in this world he may meet all kinds of trouble, and by this world's standards he may be a failure, but there awaits him a joy which this world cannot give. In the Dives and the Lazarus parable there is a picture of Dives in hell, asking mercy from Abraham. But Abraham said to him: "Son, remember that thou in thy lifetime receivedst thy good things, and likewise Lazarus evil things: but now he is comforted and thou art tormented" (Luke 16. 25).

In life two choices are always confronting a man. Will he take the course of action which will provide an immediate profit, an immediate happiness, and an immediate freedom from trouble? Or, will he take the course of action which necessitates immediate discipline, and which will provide immediate trouble, and which may mean present hardship and present persecution and present sacrifice? The Christian teaching is clear. It is the man who is prepared to accept the present toil and the present tears who will know the ultimate and permanent bliss.

iii. It may be that this Beatitude at least to some extent means that blessedness belongs to those who sorrow for the sin, the sadness and the suffering of this world. It may describe the man whose heart is touched for those who are in the midst of what Virgil called

" the tears of things ", whose sense of justice is challenged
by those who are suffering from tyranny and oppression
and injustice, to whom the appeal of weakness and
suffering and pain never comes unheard.

It is always right, according to the Christian point of
view, that a man should be detached from *things;* but it
is never right that he should be detached from *people.*
It was Jesus' teaching in the Parable of the Sheep and
the Goats (Matthew 25. 31-46) that a man's attitude to
him is seen in that man's attitude to other people. In
many ways the most unchristian of all sins is the sin of
contempt. In *The Patrician* John Galsworthy makes
Miltoun say: " The mob! How I loathe it! I hate its
mean stupidities, I hate the sound of its voice, and the
look on its face—it's so ugly, it's so little!" George
Bernard Shaw once said: " I have never had any
feeling for the working classes, except a desire to abolish
them, and to replace them by sensible people." Carlyle,
thinking of the political unwisdom of the country, once
said: " There are twenty-seven and a half million
people in this country—mostly fools."

That is the precise opposite of the teaching of Jesus,
and of the attitude of Jesus. Repeatedly it is said of Jesus
in the Gospels that he was *moved with compassion*
Mark 1. 41; 6. 34; 8. 2). The word is *splagchnizesthai,*
which is the strongest word for compassion in the Greek
language. *Splagchna* are the *bowels,* and *splagchnizesthai* means to be moved to the very depths of one's
being. The basic meaning of the Incarnation is that
God cared so intensely for men that in Jesus Christ he
deliberately chose to identify himself with the sin, the

sorrowing and the suffering of the human situation. Those whose names are written in gold letters in the honour roll of humanity are not those who looked at their fellow-men with a conscious and a contemptuous superiority, nor are they those who regarded the struggles of mankind with a cool detachment; they are those who cared so much, and who sorrowed so much, that the sorrow of their hearts drove them to spend their lives in the service of mankind. The world would be an infinitely poorer place without those who sorrowed dynamically for their fellow-men.

iv. We have not even yet come to the full depth of the meaning of this Beatitude. The real meaning of it is: "Blessed is the man who is moved to bitter sorrow at the realization of his own sin." The way to God is the way of the broken heart. Penitence is the first act of the Christian life, and penitence is sorrow. Paul said: "Godly sorrow worketh repentance to salvation" (II Corinthians 7. 10). Long before Paul, the Psalmist had said: "I will declare mine iniquity; I will be sorry for my sin" (Psalm 38. 18). The beginning of the Christian life is the utter dissatisfaction with life as it is. Augustine, telling of the days before his conversion says: "I grew more wretched, and Thou didst grow nearer."

In the spiritual biography of Paul there is a strange progression. It is likely that Galatians is the first letter which Paul ever wrote, and that he wrote it about the year A.D.48. In the first sentence of it he calls himself "Paul an apostle" (Galatians 1. 1). Without hesitation he lays claim to the highest office in the Church; it is on his possession of that office he bases his claim to write. Seven years later in the year A.D.55 he was writing to the Corinthians. There he writes: "I am the least of the apostles, and not fit to be called an apostle" (I Corinthians 15. 9). By that time he had come to think of the office of an apostle as something to which he had little right and little claim. Another eight years went by and about A.D.63 he wrote the letter called the Letter of the Ephesians, and in it he says: "Unto me who am less than the least of the saints is grace given" (Ephesians 3. 8). In the New Testament *saint* is the word for *church member* (cp. Ephesians 1. 1; Philippians 1. 1). By that time Paul had begun to think of himself, not as an apostle, but as barely fit to be a member of the Church at all. At the very end of the day, when he was awaiting death, he wrote to Timothy, and in that letter he writes: "Christ Jesus came into the world to save sinners of whom I am chief" (I Timothy 1. 15). Here the man whom all the world regarded as the supreme servant of Jesus Christ calls himself the chief of sinners. Nor is there any cause for surprise in all this.

The longer a man knows Jesus Christ, and the nearer he comes to Jesus Christ, the more two things are bound to enter into his life. First, he is bound to see more and more clearly that standard of perfection in Christ by which he must judge his own life. A man may think he does a thing well—until some day he sees a real expert doing it; and then he knows how inadequate his own standard of performance is. A man may think that he is a fairly satisfactory person, and that he has nothing to worry about—so long as he compares himself with his neighbours and with his fellow-men; but the question that the Christian has to ask is not, "Am I as good as my neighbour?" but, "Am I as good as Jesus Christ?" No human being can ever have any cause for satisfaction when the standard against which he sets himself is Jesus Christ. Such a comparison leaves him in constant mourning that he falls so far short. Second, the more a man knows Jesus Christ, the more he realizes the cost of sin. If the effect of sin was to necessitate the death on the Cross of the loveliest life which was ever lived, then sin stands revealed in all its terribleness, and a man knows that he can do nothing but mourn so long as sin has one last vestige of a place within his life.

Penitence is an attitude of mind to which a man must be reawakened every day, and, therefore, the godly sorrow of repentance is always a blessed thing, for it is the gateway to the joy of forgiveness.

But this Beatitude does not leave the matter there. To leave the matter there might well leave a man so weighted down with a sense of sin that he would be driven to despair. This Beatitude goes on to make its promise: "Blessed are they that mourn, *for they shall be comforted*." There is more in this promise than any single word can ever translate. The word which is translated *comforted* is the passive of the verb *parakalein*, which is a word with a wealth of meaning.

i. *Parakalein* does mean *to comfort* or to *console*, but it may be worth while remembering that that in fact is the rarest of all its meanings, and is not found in classical Greek at all. But beyond a doubt comfort is part of the meaning of the word here. The man who goes to God with godly sorrow for his sin will receive the comfort of God. There is a wide variety of reactions with which a penitent sinner may be received. If he goes to the one whom he has wronged to confess his sin, he may be received with adamantine implacability and turned sternly away; he may be received with a grudging concession of forgiveness which falls far short of the restoration of fellowship which true forgiveness involves; he may be received with a kind of forgiveness, a forgiveness which agrees to forgive, but which never consents to forget. There are all kinds of limitations in human forgiveness. But when a man goes to God in godly sorrow for his sin, he receives the full welcome of the love of God, and in that love his sorrow is abundantly comforted.

ii. But *parakalein* has more meanings than that. It is the word which is used for to summon to one's side as an ally, a helper, a counsellor, a witness, and it is the word which is used for to invite to a banquet. Here, then, is something more. God does not only accept and receive the sinner back again. He treats him, not as a criminal, but as an honoured guest. He does not treat him as if he could never trust him again; he invites him to become his ally, his helper, his witness among men. In the magnificence of his grace God sends us back to the field of our defeat in the certainty that his grace can turn our past defeat into future victory.

iii. *Parakalein* has a still further series of great implications. It means *to exhort* or *to encourage*. Aeschylus, for instance, uses it for troops cheering each other as they enter into battle (*Persae* 380). Aristotle uses it of stimulating and energising the mind (*Nico-machean Ethics* 1175. 7). It is used of inciting and exciting a person, and of fomenting a fire until it bursts into a flame (Xenophon, *Cyropaedia* 7. 5. 23.).

Here, then, is the greatness of the forgiveness of God. When a man goes to God with the godly sorrow of repentance, he is not comforted only with the joy of past sins forgiven and forgotten; his heart is filled with courage; his mind is stimulated to new thought and new understanding and new adventure; the flickering flame of his life is fanned to a flame. His whole life is caught up into the strength and the beauty of God.

Blessed are they that mourn for they shall be comforted. There is blessedness in sorrow; there is blessedness in taking the right way even when the right way is the hard way; there is blessedness in sorrow for the sins and the sorrows and the sufferings of men; there is supreme blessedness in the godly sorrow which leads to that repentance which receives the forgiveness of God. And when that forgiveness comes, there is comfort for the remorse of the heart, there is the glory of being trusted on the field of our defeat, there is the encouragement, the stimulus, the flame in life which God alone can give.

THE BLISS OF THE DISCIPLINED SELF

Blessed are the meek, for they shall inherit the earth (MATTHEW 5. 5).

The real greatness of this Beatitude is hidden from modern eyes, because the word *meek* has come down in the world. To modern ears it describes a weak, flabby, milk and water, spineless creature, lacking in all virility, submissive and subservient to a fault, unable to stand up for himself or for anyone else. But that is very far from the original meaning of the word. The meaning of the word is, in fact, so great and so comprehensive that it defies translation.

The word is *praus*, and it has a double ancestry, and its two ancestries look in different directions. One of them looks to God and one of them looks to men. One of them has to do mainly with a man's attitude to God; the other has to do mainly with a man's attitude to his fellow-men.

The first ancestry of the word is its Hebrew ancestry. *Praus* is the word which is used to translate the Hebrew word *anaw*. In the Authorised Version *anaw* is translated *humble, lowly* and *meek*. It is a favourite word in the Psalms, and it describes the man, who in loving and obedient humility accepts the guidance of God and the providence of God, and who never grows resentful and bitter about anything which life may bring to him, in the certainty that God's way is always best, and that God is always working all things together for good. In the Psalms such a man is very dear to God, and stands in a very special relationship to God. God hears the desire of the *humble,* and never forgets their cry (Psalm 9. 12; 10. 17; 34. 2; 69. 32). God scorns the scorners but gives grace to the *lowly;* it is better to be of a humble spirit with the lowly than to divide the spoil with the proud (Proverbs 3. 34; 16. 19). The *meek* shall eat and be satisfied (Psalm 22. 26). God guides the *meek* in justice, and teaches them his way (Psalm 25. 9). God rises in judgment to save the *meek* of the earth; he lifts up the *meek* but casts down the wicked; he pleads the cause of the *meek;* he beautifies the *meek* with salvation; the *meek* shall increase their joy in the Lord (Psalm 25. 9; 76. 9; 147. 6; 149. 4; Isaiah 11. 4; 29. 19). It may well be that arrogant men will oppress the *meek* (Amos 2. 7); but it is God's promise that the *meek* will inherit the earth (Psalm 37. 11).

In Hebrew thought the man who is *meek, anaw,* is the man who obediently accepts God's guidance, who humbly accepts whatever God sends, and who is, therefore, dear to God, and whose life is strengthened and beautified by the gifts which God can give only to such a man.

When we turn to the Greek ancestry of the word *praus,* we find an equal wealth of meaning.

We begin by noting a simple, but very significant, use of the word *praus.* It is used, as is the corresponding

Latin word *mitis*, to aescribe an animal which has been tamed and domesticated and which has become subject to control. It is, for instance, used of a horse which has been broken in and which has become obedient to the reins, and of a sheep-dog who has been trained by kindness to understand and to obey every word of command. Even from this we can see that *praus* describes that which is *under control*.

It is Aristotle who deals at length and repeatedly with the quality of *praotes,* and with the man who can be called *praus*. It was Aristotle's practice to describe every virtue as the mean between two extremes. On the one hand there was an extreme of excess; on the other there was an extreme of defect; and in between there is the virtue itself. So on the one hand there is *recklessness;* on the other hand there is *cowardice;* and between them there is the mean which is *courage*. So, then, Aristotle says that *praotes* is " the observance of the mean in relation to anger " (*Nicomachean Ethics* 4. 5. 1). It is the mean, the correct and happy medium, between excessive anger and excessive angerlessness. On the one hand there is the man who is mean and small spirited; on the other hand there is the man who is irascible, passionate, bitter, and harsh-tempered; and in between there is the man who is *praus*. The man who is *praus* " feels anger on the right grounds, against the right persons, in the right manner, at the right moment, and for the right length of time." Such an attitude of mind becomes angry "only in such a manner, for such causes, and for such a length of time as principle may ordain " (*Nicomachean Ethics* 4. 5. 3). In the *Eudemian*

Ethics (3. 3. 4) the man who is *praus* is defined as "neither too hasty- nor too slow-tempered. He does not become angry with those he ought not to, nor fail to become angry with whom he ought." The little tract on *Virtues and Vices* (4. 3) says: "To *praotes* belongs the ability to bear reproaches and slights with moderation, and not to embark on revenge quickly, and not to be easily provoked to anger, but to be free from bitterness and contentiousness, having tranquillity and stability in the spirit."

To all this we must add two other facts about the Greek view of this virtue of *praotes*.

It is the virtue of the man who acts with gentleness, when he has it in his power to act with stern severity. So it is used of a king who might have exercised vengeance on a rebellious people but who treated them with kindliness. It is used of a ruler who might have dispensed strict justice, but who dispensed forgiveness. It is used of a commander who might have dealt with an erring subordinate with unsparing discipline, but who used a sympathetic leniency. The man who is *praus* is the man who, as Browning said, knows well that it is good to have a giant's strength, but it is tyrannous to use it like a giant.

In Greek thought the virtue of *praotes* is again and again associated with *strength*. *Praotes* is not the gentleness which has its source in weakness, or in indifference, or in fear, or in a slack and unprincipled tolerance. It is the gentleness of strength. So when men spoke of Cyrus, as Xenophon tells us, "one spoke of his wisdom, another of his strength, another of his *gentleness* (*praotes*), and another of his beauty and of his commanding presence." In Plato the character of the guardian of the state is sketched. Such a man must treat his friends with *gentleness* and his foes with sternness. He must be *gentle* and spirited. He must have the passion which will right wrong and challenge injustice, but he must have the *gentleness,* which will see in the wrong-doer a sick man to be healed, and an erring mortal to be restored to the right way. So, then, *praus* signifies strength and gentleness combined.

Praus, meek, has in it an attitude to God and an attitude to men.

In its Godward look it describes the man who gives to God the perfect trust, the perfect obedience, and the perfect submission. It is the attitude of Job when he said: "The Lord gave, and the Lord hath taken away; blessed be the name of the Lord" (Job 1. 21). "Though he slay me yet will I trust him" (Job 13. 15). It is the attitude of Mary, the mother of Jesus, when she said: "Behold the handmaid of the Lord; be it unto me according to thy word" (Luke 1. 38). It is the attitude of Paul, when, all resistance broken, he said: "Lord, what wilt thou have me do?" (Acts 9. 6). It is the attitude of the hymn-writer, when he said:

> My times are in thy hand:
> Why should I doubt or fear?
> My Father's hand will never cause
> His child a needless tear.

It is the attitude of Jesus when he said: "Not as I will, but as thou wilt. Thy will be done" (Matthew 26. 39, 42). It is the attitude of the man who in every age finds what Aristotle called "tranquillity and stability" in committing himself into the hands of God.

In its manward look this Beatitude in effect says: "Blessed is the man who is always angry at the right time and who is never angry at the wrong time." "Be angry and sin not," said Paul (Ephesians 4. 26). Anger is one of God's greatest gifts to men. But anger is like a strong medicine, which if it is used in the right way, can do infinite good, and which, if it is used in the wrong way, can do infinite harm. What, then, is the rule for anger? When anger is for our own sake, it is always wrong. When anger is for the sake of others, it is often divinely right. When we look at Jesus, we never see him angry at the slights, the insults, the injuries which he himself received. But we see his eyes glint with anger, as he looked round on the coldly orthodox Scribes and Pharisees who placed the observance of the details of the Sabbath law above the healing of a man with a withered hand (Mark 3. 5). We see his eyes blaze with anger when he saw the money-changers and the sellers of doves making an iniquitous profit out of the poor pilgrims in the Temple Court, for it was there that the Christ of love became the Christ of the whip (Matthew 21. 12; Mark 11. 15; Luke 19. 45; John 2. 14, 15).

To be right anger must be selfless anger. It must be an anger which is not destructive but saving, not lacerating but healing. The world would be a poorer place without the power of righteous anger, and it is precisely that anger that the man who is *meek, praus,* possesses in his heart.

Every word to be fully understood must become flesh;

every great virtue and quality to be fully demonstrated must be incarnated in a person. It is so with this quality of meekness. In the Bible the quality of meekness is connected specially with two people. It was said of Moses that he was very *meek*, above all men which were on the face of the earth (Numbers 12. 3). It was Jesus' claim for himself: "I am *meek* and lowly in heart" (Matthew 11. 29). History has never seen a leader with more strength and force of character than Moses, nor a leader with a greater gift of righteous anger, when there was occasion for it. The world has never seen more dynamic power than the power which throbbed in the personality of the man Jesus of Nazareth. That is the meekness which is blessed.

To the meek a promise is made, and the promise is that "they will inherit the earth." This Beatitude is a direct quotation of Psalm 37. 11, so it will be to the Old Testament that we must first go in order to interpret its meaning.

The word *inherit* has in the Bible a different meaning from the meaning in which we commonly use it. We commonly use the word to mean to enter into possession of something which has been left in a will; but in the Bible the word usually means to enter into possession of something which has been promised and foretold by God. Further, it will help us to see the original meaning of this phrase, if we remember that it can be equally well translated: "The meek shall inherit *the land*." This promise has three stages in it.

i. Originally it had to do with the entering of the children of Israel into the promised land. God had promised Abraham that he would give him the promised land to inherit it (Genesis 15. 7). It was God's promise that he would give to the Jews the land of Palestine as an inheritance (Deuteronomy 4. 38). So, originally this was a promise that if the children of Israel were obedient to God, if they committed their ways to him to trust him and to obey him, then one day they would enter into the land which he had promised them, and that they would dwell there in prosperity and peace. The great truth behind this is that obedience and trust are the conditions of entering into possession of the promises of God. Any man who chooses to go his own way will arrive in the far country and not in the promised land.

ii. As time went on, the Jews came to see that by human means they could never become great; their nation was too small and the world was too great. So they began to look for the coming of the Messiah, the entry of God's Anointed King into the world, the coming of one who would lead them into all the bliss and the blessing of the Messianic age. So the promise of the Psalmist came to mean something greater than the possession of the land of Palestine; it came to mean that the meek, those who humbly trusted God and who obediently accepted his will, would enter into all the blessings of the Kingdom of God upon earth. It is those who spend their lives waiting upon God who will be ready for the Kingdom when it comes.

iii. But with the coming of Jesus Christ this Beatitude acquires a new width and a new greatness. For us it means far more than the possession of any territory upon earth; for us it does not mean that we have to wait for bliss and blessedness until the coming of the Messianic Age in some distant future beyond the hills of time. It means the promise of life here and now; and that promised life has two things in it.

It has *peace*. The man who has committed himself and all his ways to God has a peace that the world cannot give nor ever take away, for he knows that nothing can pluck him from the hand of God, and that no experience of life can separate him from the love of God.

It has *power*. Meekness means the mastery of anger and passion. The man who is *praus* is the man who has such self-mastery that he is always angry at the right time and never angry at the wrong time. " He that is slow to anger is better than the mighty; and he that ruleth his spirit than he that taketh a city " (Proverbs 16. 32). Self-discipline is the way to strength; self-mastery is the way to power; and he who rules himself is indeed a king among men. To have the discipline of meekness is to have the power which makes life great, for only when a man has mastered himself is he able to rule others.

And now we can take the Greek aspect of *praus* and the Hebrew aspect of *praus* and put them together. From the Hebrew point of view the man who is *praus* is committed to God in perfect obedience and in perfect trust; from the Greek point of view the man who is *praus* is the man who has every instinct and every passion under discipline and under control. Therefore, in the final analysis, the man who in peace and in power inherits life, is not the man who is *self-controlled*, for such self-control is not in man's power as all experience shows, but the man who is *God-controlled*. And so the final meaning of this Beatitude is: "O the bliss of the man who has so committed himself to God that he is entirely God-controlled, for such a man will be right with God and will be right with self and will be right with men, and will enter into that life which God has promised and which God alone can give."

THE BLISS OF THE STARVING SOUL

*Blessed are they which do hunger and thirst after
righteousness, for they shall be filled* (MATTHEW
5. 6).

It takes far more than a dictionary to define the meaning
of a word, especially when a word is a word of human
experience. When a word is a word of experience, then
the experience of him who uses it, and of those who hear
it, will define its meaning. Clearly the word *pain* means
something quite different to a person who has never
had a day's illness in his life, and to a person who has
passed through a furnace of physical agony. Clearly the
word *love* will mean something quite different to a
child of ten, a youth or a maiden of twenty, a mature
adult of middle age, an aged one who is far down the
vale of years. Words which describe an experience have a
basic meaning, but it is life which decides what the
intensity of that meaning is.

It is so with the Beatitude which tells of the bliss of the
starving soul. This saying would mean something quite
different to a Palestinian audience in the time of Jesus
from that which it means to a twentieth-century audience
which enjoys all the plenty which social and economic
development have brought. There are few in our

situation who have ever known what it is to be genuinely
hungry. In Palestine in the time of Jesus the wage of a
working-man was eightpence a day. No one ever grew
fat on that; and, if for the day labourer there was even
one day's unemployment, then actual hunger invaded the
home. Eric F. F. Bishop in *Apostles of Palestine* tells us
that even in the twentieth century one of the Com-
missions despatched to Palestine during the time of the
Mandate estimated the average income of a peasant
family at £24 a year. For a family to eat meat was in
Palestine a rare experience. In that ancient world hunger
was not something which could be satisfied with a
passing snack. It could often be the hunger which
threatened life, the starvation in which a man had to
eat or die. The same is true of thirst. There are few
in our situation who have ever known what it is to be
genuinely thirsty. We live in a situation in which
we turn a tap and water flows. In that ancient world
men were dependent on streams and wells, and there
might be a long, long distance between them on a
journey, and the water-skin might be empty. Still worse,
the sand-storm might come, and all that a man could do
was to turn his back to the swirling sand, and hide his
head in his hood, while his mouth and his throat and his
nostrils and his lungs were filled with the fine sand,
which made him choke with thirst. People who lived
in conditions like that knew the thirst which has to be
satisfied, if a man is to survive. What Jesus is saying here
is: " Blessed is the man who longs for righteousness as
a starving man longs for food, and as a man perishing of
thirst longs for water."

This is a metaphor which the psalmists and the prophets used to describe the longing of the soul for God. As the hart pants for the water brooks, so the soul of the psalmist thirsts for the living God (Psalm 42. 1, 2). The soul of the psalmist thirsts for God, as in a dry parched land where there is no water (Psalm 63. 1). The invitation of the prophet is that he who thirsts should come and take of the water of life freely (Isaiah 55. 1). Here is a picture of a time when water had to be *bought*. In *Eastern Customs in Bible Lands* H. B. Tristram tells of sitting in the Eastern bazaars, with little or no shelter from the pitiless sun and hearing " the sonorous and ceaseless cry of the water-bearer as he perambulates the narrow streets," and seeing the way-farers buying water at a *para* a drink.

Here, then, Jesus is confronting his disciples with a promise which is also a challenge and a demand. What he meant by *righteousness* we shall later have to investigate, but he is saying here: " Do you desire righteousness with that intensity of desire with which a starving man desires food, and a man parched with thirst desires water?" This is a challenge and demand with which Jesus continually confronted men. It was with this challenge that he confronted the Rich Young Ruler (Matthew 19. 16-22; Mark 10. 17-22; Luke 18. 18-23). The young man came to Jesus pleading to be enabled to find eternal life, real life. He was an attractive character for, when Jesus looked at him, he loved him. In answer to Jesus' questions he claimed that he had kept all the commandments from his youth upwards. Jesus then confronted him with the demand that he should go and sell all that he had and give the proceeds to the poor. In effect Jesus was saying to him : "Do you want eternal life as much as that? Are you prepared to sacrifice the luxuries of this life to gain eternal life?" And, when the matter was put that way, the young man went sorrowfully away. It was with this challenge that Jesus confronted one of the men who wished to follow him. The man said that he would follow Jesus anywhere. Jesus answered : "Foxes have holes, and birds of the air have nests; but the Son of Man hath not where to lay his head" (Luke 9. 57, 58). In effect Jesus said to that man : "Do you want to follow me enough to face a life like that?" It was with this challenge that Jesus confronted his disciples when he told them that they must love him more than father or mother or any other of their kith and kin (Matthew 10. 37; Luke 14. 26). In effect he said to them : "Do you want to become my disciple enough to give me the unconditional first place in your life?" In view of all this this Beatitude has four things to say about the Christian life.

i. It uncompromisingly lays down the demand of the Christian life. This is the most demanding of the Beatitudes; it insists that the Christian life is not for the dilettante; it is not even for the interested and the attracted; it is for those who desire righteousness as a matter of life and death. In the novel *Quo Vadis?* there is a picture of a young Roman called Vinicius. He is in love with a Christian girl, but because he is a pagan she will not return his love. Without her knowledge he followed her to the little secret gathering of the Christians, and there he heard Peter preach. As he

listened something happened within him. He knew that
Jesus Christ was the most important reality in life, but,
" He felt that, if he wished to follow that teaching, he
would have to place on a burning pile all his thoughts,
habits and character, his whole nature up to that moment,
burn them into ashes, and then fill himself with a life
altogether different, and an entirely new soul." That is
the demand of Christianity. The Christian does not say:
" I am interested in Christ." He says: " For me to live
is Christ " (Philippians 1. 21). He does not say: " I
would like to come to terms and to some arrangement
with this Jesus." He says: "I surrender to Jesus
Christ."

ii. By implication it lays down the main cause of
failure in the Christian life. That cause of failure is
simply that we do not sufficiently desire to be a
Christian. It is the experience of life that, if a man
desires a thing sufficiently, he will get it. If he is
prepared to bend every energy, to sacrifice everything,
to toil with sufficient intensity, to wait with sufficient
patience, he will succeed in getting that on which he has
set his heart. The great barrier to our becoming fully
Christian is our failure to desire it enough, our deep-
rooted unwillingness to pay the price of it, our fundamental desire not to upset life, but to keep it as it is.
Luke gives us a different, and a complementary, version
of this Beatitude: " Woe unto you that are full! for
ye shall hunger " (Luke 6. 25). That means: " Woe
unto you who are satisfied, who are content with
things as they are, who have no passionate desire
for that which you have not got. You may live

comfortably enough just now, but the day comes
when you will discover that you have somehow
missed the greatest things of all." In *The Master of
Ballantrae* Robert Louis Stevenson describes how the
master left the ancestral home at Durrisdeer for the last
time. He had not been a good man, but in that moment
he was sad. He turned to his steward McKellar. "Ah,
McKellar," he said, "do you think I have never a
regret?" "I do not think," said McKellar, "that you
could be so bad a man unless you had all the machinery
to be a good one." "Not all," said the master, "it is
there you are in error—the malady of not wanting."
The biggest barrier to the full entry into the Christian
life is nothing other than the malady of not wanting—
and that is what this Beatitude lays down.

iii. We have already said that this is the most
demanding of all the Beatitudes; but it is also the kindest
and most encouraging of the Beatitudes. It is the
Beatitude which tells us of the sympathy of God for
the struggler on the Christian way. It is not he
who has *attained* righteousness, who is called blessed,
but he who *hungers and thirsts for it*. If the blessedness
was for those who had achieved, it would be for none;
but it is not for those who achieve in this case, it is for
those who long. The mystery of man is not the sin of
man; the mystery of man is the goodness of man. In
man there is an instinctive love of goodness, and an
instinctive power to recognise it. It is easy to cite on the
other hand the great evil men of history, the men who
seem to have been born without any moral sense, without
pity and without compassion; but, if we take the ordinary

run of men, there is in man an instinctive recognition of, and desire for, goodness.

In his autobiography H. G. Wells drew a contrast between "the secret splendour of our intentions," and the poverty of our achievements. "A man may be a bad musician," he says, "and yet be passionately in love with music." Thomas à Kempis said: "Man sees the deed, but God sees the intention." And that applies in both directions. God does not see only the mixed and impure motive that may lurk behind that which looks like a good deed; he also sees the longing for goodness and the love of goodness which lies behind the sins and the mistakes of life. Sir Norman Birkett, as he then was, the great lawyer and judge, looking back on the many criminals he had met once said: "They are condemned to some nobility; all their lives long the desire for good is at their heels, the implacable hunter." Robert Louis Stevenson spoke of those who had made shipwreck of life "clutching the remnants of virtue in the brothel or on the scaffold". When David wished to build a house unto God, it was not given to him to do so—that was reserved for his son Solomon—but nevertheless God said to him: "Thou didst well that it was in thine heart" (I Kings 8. 18). This Beatitude blesses not only the deed, but also the dream that never came true.

iv. It may well be that this Beatitude tells us of the totality of Christian goodness. It is quite true that in later Greek, such as the Greek of the New Testament, the grammatical niceties of the classical period break down; but there is in this Beatitude a grammatical point which may well be of the greatest importance. In classical Greek verbs of hungering and thirsting normally take the genitive case after them; the genitive case is the case which we express by the word *of*. In the phrase, " a slice of bread ", *of bread* is the genitive case. The reason for this grammatical usage is that normally we hunger and thirst for part of some supply of food or drink. We do not want the whole loaf; we want a part *of the loaf*. We do not want the whole pitcher; we want some *of the water* which is in the pitcher. But, when these verbs do take the direct accusative, it means that the person involved wants *all* the food and *all* the drink there is. If a Greek said, "I hunger for bread," or, "I thirst for water," and the words *bread* and *water* were in the accusative case, it would mean that he wanted the whole loaf, and the entire contents of the pitcher. In this Beatitude *righteousness* is in the accusative case; and, therefore, if we are to translate this with strict accuracy, we ought to translate it: "Blessed are those who hunger and thirst for *all of righteousness,* for total righteousness."

That is what so seldom happens. There are people against whose moral character no possible fault can be found; they are completely respectable; intemperance, gambling, adultery, swearing, dishonesty, failure to pay their debts could never possibly be attributed to them; but they are cold and hard and without sympathy. No one who had made a mistake could lay his head on their shoulder, and sob out his sorry story. They are good, but they are cold. On the other hand there are people who have all kinds of faults; they may drink to excess; their language may at times be lurid; their

passions are not always under control; it is easy to point
at their moral errors and their failure in the respectable
virtues. But, if anyone else is in trouble, they would give
him the coat off their back, and hand him their last penny
without a thought of grudging it. Their morals may
be erratic, but their heart is warm. The truth is that in
neither of these cases can you say that these people are
good in the full sense of the term. Each of them has a
part of goodness, but not the *whole* of it; each has
fragmentary, but not *total* goodness. The Christian
goodness is a complete goodness in which virtue and
love join hands.

We have not yet sought to define what this word
righteousness means. The word is *dikaiosune*, and it has
three meanings which are all possible, and all relevant.
It means *justice*; it means *righteousness* in the sense of
right-living; and it is the word which is used for the
justification which comes by faith. Let us look at it
in each of these three senses.

i. *Blessed are those who hunger and thirst for justice*.
This burning desire for justice may move in two
directions. (a) There are those who urgently and
intensely desire justice for themselves, and for the cause
for which they stand. There are those who are conscious
of their own rectitude, conscious of their own complete
commitment to Jesus Christ, and for whom life has been
an agonising thing, but who yet refuse to believe that that
is the end of the story. In the Revelation the souls of the
martyrs cry out to God, asking how long it will be
before he vindicates them (Revelation 6. 10). Such a
desire for justice, such a confidence in the justice and in

the honour of God, such a refusal to be driven to despair by the events of time, is the demonstration of complete trust in the power and will of God to vindicate in time or in eternity those who entrusted all things to him. This is the spirit of the man who can say: "I know whom I have believed, and am persuaded that he is able to keep that which I have committed unto him against that day" (II Timothy 1. 12). "I believe," said Robert Louis Stevenson, "in an ultimate decency of things, and, if I woke up in hell, I would still believe in it."

(b) There are those who urgently and intensely desire justice, not so much for themselves, as for those who are suffering from injustice. This has been the motive of all the great social reformers. J. E. McFadyen entitled the book of Amos "A Cry for Social Justice". Amos is appalled and enraged by the robbery and violence which have their homes in great houses, and by those who take bribes and refuse justice to the poor (Amos 3. 10, 12). His anger is hot against those who swallow up the needy, those who give short measure, and who overcharge even for that, in their lust for profit, those who accept the very bodies of the poor in payment of their debts (Amos 8. 4-6). There are those who have had such a hunger and thirst for justice that they could never be content in a civilization in which the law is weighted in favour of one colour or one class; in a society in which the few have too much and the many too little; in an economic system in which men are treated, not as persons, but as things.

It is true that those who intensely desire justice that

God's cause may be vindicated, and who urgently seek for justice for those to whom life is unjust, are blessed.

ii. *Blessed are those who hunger and thirst for righteousness.* In Greek ethics *dikaiosune* was a great word; it is the virtue of the man who is constantly observant of his duty to the gods and his duty to men. In Greek the man who is *dikaios* is the man who pays what he owes to the gods and to men. In this sense righteousness is that love of God, which issues in complete trust and absolute obedience; and that love of men, which issues in selfless service and unwearied forgiveness.

Blessed indeed is the man whose most passionate desire is to love God and to love men as he ought.

iii. *Blessed are those who hunger and thirst for justification.* In Paul *dikaiosune* is what we know as justification by faith. The Greek verb which is translated *to justify* is *dikaioun.* It does not mean to find reasons why a man is right, as it does in English. It does not even mean to make a man just. It means to treat and to accept a man as a just and a good man. When God justifies the sinner, God in his mercy and grace accepts the sinner as if he was a good man. Clearly this at once introduces a new relationship between God and man. So long as we think of God as the stern and inexorable judge and law-giver, there can be nothing between us and God but distance, estrangement and fear. But once we know that God is ready to accept us and to love us and to forgive us just as we are, the distance is replaced my intimacy, the estrangement by friendship, the fear by loving and grateful trust. This is justification by faith; and, therefore, the basic and essential meaning of justification is *a right relationship with God*. To be justified is to be in a right relationship with God; and justification is such a relationship. So, then, if we take this meaning this Beatitude will mean; "Blessed is the man whose most intense desire is to enter into a right relationship with God."

It is not necessary that we should choose between these meanings. We may well believe that this Beatitude includes all these things, and that the hunger and thirst of which it speaks are for the vindication of the cause of God and for justice for all men; for that personal righteousness which loves and obeys God and serves and forgives men; for that right relationship with God in which all the fear and the estrangement have turned into confidence and trust. No man could hunger and thirst for any greater gifts than these.

After the affirmation there comes the promise. "Blessed are they that hunger and thirst after righteousness; *for they shall be filled.*" The word which is used for *filled* is an extraordinary word. It is the word *chortazesthai*. Originally this word was used to describe the special fattening of animals for killing. When it did come to be used of men, it meant to stuff a person full to the point of complete satiety. It always remained something of a colloquial word, and it always retained something of the idea of filling a person full to repletion. If a man hungers and thirsts for that righteousness which God alone can give, God will not send him empty away, but God will fill him, until his longings are achieved and his soul is satisfied.

THE BLISS OF THE KIND HEART

Blessed are the merciful, for they shall obtain mercy
(MATTHEW 5. 7).

This Beatitude has to be set against two backgrounds;
it has to be set against the background of the Old
Testament, and it has to be set against the background of
the contemporary world in which it was spoken.

Mercy, *chesedh*, is one of the great words of the Old
Testament. In the Old Testament it occurs more than one
hundred and fifty times, and on more than nine-tenths of
the occasions when it does occur the reference is to
God and to the action of God. Great as the word mercy
is, it may be that the use of this word mercy to translate
chesedh has done something to narrow and to belittle its
meaning. For the most part we think of mercy in terms
of the remission of penalty, or the relaxing of a demand
which might have been enforced. In ordinary usage, to
have mercy upon a man is to agree not to treat him with
the sternness and the severity and the rigorous justice
which he deserves. But *chesedh* is a far more positive
thing than that. *Chesedh* is translated *mercy* ninety-six
times in the Authorised Version, but it is also translated
kindness no fewer than thirty-eight times, and it is
kindness which is the basic idea of the word. *Chesedh*,

when it is used of God, is the outgoing kindness of the heart of God. It is the basis of God's whole relationship to man, and especially of his relationship to his people Israel.

It is to God that mercy belongs (Isaiah 62. 12), and it is in mercy that God delights (Micah 7. 18). The mercy of God is so infinite that it reaches the heavens (Psalm 36. 5; 57. 10), and it is so enduring that it lasts for ever (Psalm 89. 1, 2; 100. 5; 103. 17). One of the most often repeated of all statements in the Old Testament is that the mercy of God endureth for ever (I Chronicles 16. 34; II Chronicles 7. 3; Ezra 3. 11; Psalm 106. 1; 107. 1 138. 8; twenty-six times in Psalm 136; Jeremiah 33. 11).

This mercy of God is demonstrated in the events of history. It is to be seen in the deliverance from Egypt (Exodus 15. 13), and in the kindness of the Persian king, when he allowed the exiles to return to Jerusalem (Ezra 9. 9).

Not only is God's mercy demonstrated in the events of history, it is to be seen in nature and in the very structure of the world. The earth is full of the mercy of God (Psalm 119. 64), and it is in the mercy of God that the rain and the sunshine come (Job 37. 13).

Wherever a man looks, to the events of history or to the processes of nature, he is confronted with the outgoing mercy of God. It is this mercy which decides all man's relationships with God. It is the ground of man's appeal to God in the time of trouble. " Save me," cries the Psalmist, " for thy mercy's sake " (Psalm 6. 4; 31. 16; 49. 26). It is the ground of man's appeal for forgiveness when he knows that he has sinned and disobeyed God. It is to the fact that God is long-suffering and of great mercy that Moses appeals for forgiveness for the perversity of the people (Numbers 14. 18, 19). The Psalmist lifts up his soul to God, because God is plenteous in mercy (Psalm 86. 5). It is the ground of the trust and the serenity of the good man. The Psalmist has trusted in God's mercy (Psalm 13. 5; 52. 8), and he knows that through the mercy of God he will not be moved (Psalm 21. 7). It is the mercy of God which gives a good man hope (Psalm 33. 18; 57. 3; 59. 10; 90. 14). It is the mercy of God which gives him joy, even in the day of his trouble (Psalm 31. 7). It is the ground of the assurance with which the good man meets life. From heaven God sends his mercy and his truth to save (Psalm 57. 3; 61. 7). It is the ground of the gratitude of the good man to God. The Psalmist sings of God's mercy, for God has been his defence in the time of trouble (Psalm 59. 16). It is through the mercy of God that prayer is heard (Psalm 66. 20). That mercy of God can and does deliver even from death and the grave (Psalm 86. 13). That mercy is the source of the good man's strength, for it is it which upheld him when his foot slipped (Psalm 94. 18).

When we examine the occurrences of the word mercy in the Old Testament we find that it is connected with what the Authorised Version calls *truth* oftener than with anything else. God did not leave Abraham destitute of his mercy and his truth (Genesis 24. 27). The paths of the Lord, as the Psalmist has found, are mercy and truth (Psalm 25. 10; 36. 5; 57. 3; 61. 7; 89. 14; 98. 3; 115. 1). The word for *truth* is *emeth;* and it does not mean intellectual truth; it means *steadfastness* and complete *fidelity* to a promise. So, then, the mercy and the truth of God go together. The outgoing love of God is no capricious thing, changing, as it were, with the mood of God; it is something on which men can absolutely depend because it is founded on the fidelity and the steadfastness of God to himself and to his promises.

That is why again and again the mercy of God is connected with the lives of the great characters in the Old Testament story. It was in the mercy of God that Lot escaped from Sodom (Genesis 19. 19). Jacob sees his life directed and kept by the mercy of God (Genesis 32. 10). It was the mercy of God which directed Joseph's amazing rise to success when he was sold as a slave boy into Egypt (Genesis 39. 21). It is the mercy of God which is with David the king, and which gives him a son to succeed him (II Samuel 7. 15; 22. 51; I Kings 3. 6). It is the mercy of God which has directed the history of Israel (Psalm 106. 7). In every case these men who made history would have said with the hymn-writer:

> With mercy and with judgment
> My web of time He wove.

We have now seen that this *chesedh*, this mercy, is specially connected with the fidelity and the steadfastness of God, and with God's direction of the lives of his servants and his people. Here we come to the basic and the essential characteristic of the relationship of which *chesedh* is the expression. In more than twelve places in the Old Testament the word *mercy* is connected with the word *covenant*. God is the faithful God who keeps *covenant and mercy* with those who love him (Deuter-

onomy 7. 9). The Psalmist hears God say of his
Anointed King: "My mercy will I keep for him for
evermore, and my covenant shall stand fast with him"
(Psalm 89. 28). The ideas of *mercy* and *covenant* are
inseparably connected. The idea of the covenant is basic
to the whole Old Testament. The covenant means that
God graciously entered into a special relationship with
the people of Israel, a relationship in which he would
be their God and they would be his people, a relationship
which was initiated by God alone, but which is to be
maintained by the obedience of the people to the Law
which God had given them (Exodus 24. 1-8). In that
covenant relationship *chesedh* is God's attitude to his
beloved people. *Chesedh* is God's steadfast and faithful
adherence to his special relationship to his own people;
it is the outgoing love of God to his people within that
special relationship into which he entered with them, and
to which he will never be false. That is why Sir George
Adam Smith very beautifully translated *chesedh* "leal
love". *Chesedh* is the loyal outgoing love of God to
his own people.

It is exactly in this relationship that we have the
explanation of another aspect of this mercy. It is,
of course, true in one sense to say that outgoing love of
God goes out to all men; but at the same time it is also
true that in another sense there are certain conditions
to be fulfilled. The condition of the covenant was that
the people should obey and serve the Law of God. The
Law was read to them and the people said: "All that
the Lord hath said will we do, and be obedient" (Exodus
24. 7). Therefore, again and again in the Old Testament

we find that this mercy is specially to those who love God and who keep his commandments (Exodus 20. 6; Deuteronomy 5. 10; 7. 9). It it to those who walk before the Lord with their whole heart (I Kings 8. 23). It is to such as keep his commandments and his testimonies (Psalm 25. 10). It is towards them that fear him (Psalm 103. 11), and to them that devise good (Proverbs 14. 22). God's loyalty is doubly rich in its gifts to those who are loyal to him.

Since this *chesedh*, this mercy, is the characteristic of God in his relationship with men, it is only to be expected that God wishes this mercy to be the characteristic of men's relationships with each other, and there is always condemnation for the man who fails to reproduce it in his life. It is the complaint and condemnation of the Psalmist that the wicked remembered not to show mercy (Psalm 109. 16). The warning of the wise man is, " Let not mercy and truth forsake thee " (Proverbs 3. 3). It is the charge of Hosea that there is no truth, nor mercy, nor knowledge of God in the land (Hosea 4. 1). He warns men to observe mercy and justice (Hosea 12. 6), and he warns them that nothing, not even sacrifice, can take the place of mercy in the sight of God (Hosea 6. 6). Micah sums up the whole duty of man in the commandments to do justice, to love mercy, and to walk humbly before God (Micah 6. 8), and Zechariah appeals for justice, mercy and love toward our brother (Zechariah 7. 9).

In the Old Testament mercy is no negative thing; it is not merely the agreement to suspend judgment, to remit penalty, to mitigate justifiable and deserved severity. It is the outgoing love of God to his covenant people, a love to which God is pledged and to which he will be for ever true, a love which is seen in the processes of nature and in the events of history, a love on which the whole relationship of man and God depend, an outgoing love which men must reproduce in their relationships with each other.

In the Greek of the New Testament the Hebrew *chesedh* becomes *eleos*. The word is not so common in the New Testament; it occurs twenty-seven times. But the use of it is highly significant.

God is rich in mercy (Ephesians 2. 4), and it is that mercy which saved us (Titus 3. 5). It is that mercy which we find at the throne of grace (Hebrews 4. 16); it is that mercy which gives us hope through the Resurrection of Jesus Christ (I Peter 1. 3), and through which Jesus Christ confers eternal life upon us (Jude 21). A particularly significant usage of it is that Paul connects the mercy of God with the giving of the gospel to the Gentiles (Romans 9. 23; 11. 31; 15. 9). The outgoing love of God has gone even further out and has embraced, not only the people of the original covenant, but all mankind.

We do not find the word often on the lips of Jesus, but the importance he attached to it is clear. Twice Jesus quotes the saying of Hosea, that God wants mercy and not sacrifice (Hosea 6. 6; Matthew 9. 13; 12. 27). His condemnation of the Pharisees is that they have been meticulous about the details of the ceremonial law, and have forgotten the great essentials—justice, mercy and faith (Matthew 23. 23). The Parable of the Good

Samaritan is mercy in action, and all are bidden to go and to imitate that mercy (Luke 10. 37). It is clear that Jesus too saw this outgoing love as the great characteristic of the relationships of the Christian with his fellow-men.

We must now set this Beatitude against its second background, against the background of the pagan world in which it was first spoken. A Christless world is a callous world, and mercy was never a characteristic of pagan life. Sir Henry Holland, the famous medical missionary from Quetta, whose work on eye troubles is world famous, tells how sometimes a patient would be brought in, in whom the trouble was so far advanced that his eyes were beyond the help of surgery. When he had to break news like that to a patient, the by-standers would roar with laughter, and tell the patient to begone and not to be a nuisance to the doctor. Sympathy was unknown. One of Mary Slessor's most heart-breaking problems in Calabar was the fact that the Africans dreaded twins, as being of evil omen. They were never allowed to live; they were killed, crushed into an earthenware pot, and flung to the leopards to devour. A world without Christ is a world without mercy. Let us look at certain of the merciless elements in the world of New Testament times.

The Jew was merciless to the sinner and merciless to the Gentile. As Jesus saw it, there is joy in heaven over one sinner who repents (Luke 15. 7, 10); as the Jewish teachers saw it, "There is joy before God when those who provoke him perish from the world." Jesus believed in salvation; the Jews believed in obliteration. It is true that some Jewish teachers held that the poor of the

Gentiles must be helped, their sick visited, and their dead
buried equally with Jews; but that was not orthodox
belief. According to the Law it was forbidden to help a
Gentile mother and her child even in the crisis of child-
birth. If a Jew had become a renegade from the faith, it
was not even lawful to summon medical attention for
him, even if his life was in danger. The Gentiles were to
be killed as snakes are crushed; they were created for no
other purpose than to be fuel for the fires of Hell. There
is little mercy there.

In the Roman world life was merciless especially
to the slave and to the child. The slave, as Aristotle said
(*Nicomachean Ethics* 8. 11. 6) was no different from a
living tool, and what consideration can a tool receive? A
master could, and did, kill his slave, as when Vedius
Pollio flung his slave to the savage lampreys in the
fishpool of his courtyard, because he had stumbled and
broken a goblet (Pliny, *Natural History* 9. 23). It is
Cato's advice when he writes on agriculture: "When
you take possession of a farm, look over the livestock and
hold a sale. Sell your oil, if the price is satisfactory, and
sell the surplus of your wine and grain. Sell worn-out
oxen, blemished cattle and sheep, wool, hides, an old
wagon, old tools, an old slave, a sickly slave, and
whatever else is superfluous" (*On Agriculture* 2. 7).
Juvenal tells of the haughty mistress being dressed by her
slave-girl for an appointment. "Why is this curl
standing up?" she asks, and then down comes a thong of
bull's hide to inflict chastisement for the offending
ringlet (*Satires* 6. 486-492). There are masters who
"delight in the sound of a cruel flogging, thinking it

sweeter than the sirens' song", who are never happy "until they have summoned a torturer and can brand someone with a red hot iron for stealing a couple of towels", who "revel in clanking chains" (Juvenal, *Satires* 14. 16-22). Of course there were kindly masters, but officially, so to speak, there was no such thing as sympathy for a slave, who was not even a human being.

The ancient world practised the exposure of children. The unwanted child was simply thrown out like refuse. Hilarion writes to his wife Alis in 1 B.C. with the strangest mixture of love and callousness:

Hilarion to his wife Alis, warmest greetings. . . .
I want you to know that we are still in Alexandria.
Don't worry if, when they all go home, I stay on in
Alexandria. I beg and entreat you, take care of the
little child; and, as soon as we get our pay, I will
send it up to you. If—good luck to you!—you bear
a child, if it is a boy, let it live; if it is a girl, throw it
out. You told Aphrodisias to tell me, "Don't forget
me." How can I possibly forget you. Don't worry.

The exposure of an unwanted child was normal routine. In Stobaeus (*Eclogues* 75) there is a saying: "The poor man raises his sons, but the daughters, if one is poor, we expose."

An exposed child might be picked up and trained for the brothels, or, worse, it might be deliberately maimed, and then used by some professional beggar to awaken the sympathy and extract the alms of the passers-by.

The child who was weak or sickly or ill-formed had little chance of survival. In the *Republic* (460 B) Plato insists that only the children of better unions must be kept, and any defective child must be done away with. "Let there be a law," says Aristotle, "that no deformed child shall be reared" (*Politics* 7. 14. 10). Even Seneca lays it down: "Mad dogs we knock on the head; the fierce and savage ox we slay; sickly sheep we put to the knife to keep them from infecting the flock; unnatural progeny we destroy; we drown even children who at birth are weakly and abnormal. It is not anger but reason which separates the harmful from the sound" (*On Anger*, 1. 15. 2). The sheer callousness of the pagan world is almost inconceivable to a world which has known Christian mercy.

As a last example of the failure of mercy in the pagan world, we take the text on which all the great Greek tragic dramas were written—"The doer shall suffer." It was the Greek conviction that from the moment a man did a wrong thing Nemesis was on his heels, and would not rest until the man was destroyed. It was the Greek conviction that the whole universe was designed to smash the sinner. A God of mercy was beyond their ken.

Here, then, is the background against which Jesus spoke of the bliss of the merciful. What did he mean by this mercy which the Christian is to show in his life and in his relationships with his fellow-men? The essence of the whole matter is that the merciful are those who bear towards others that outgoing love which reflects and reproduces the outgoing love of God. To be merciful is to have the same attitude to men as God has, to think of men as God thinks of them, to feel for men as God feels for them, to act towards men as God acts towards them. Clement of Alexandria once made the startling statement that the true Christian Gnostic "practises being God"; and that is exactly what being merciful means. Let us, then, more closely define this mercy.

First and foremost, this mercy is *outgoing* love. If it is outgoing, it is necessarily first *outlooking*. Mercy is the reverse of self-centredness; it is something which the man who concentrates on himself can never possess in his heart and can never show in his life. It is the antithesis of selfishness. It is the attitude of the man for whom the needs of others are more clamant than his own, and the sorrows of others more poignant than his own. This mercy is not possible so long as a man consciously or unconsciously regards himself as the centre of the universe. As Nels Ferré has said in *Christ and the Christian*: "The Church is the fellowship of the dead-to-themselves and the alive-for-Christ." Mercy comes when love of self is replaced by love of God and love of man, which are the fulfilment of both the great commandment of Jesus Christ and of the life of Jesus Christ.

This mercy is necessarily an *individualised* outgoing love. It is not a vague generalised benevolence. A sentimental love of humanity can often go hand in hand with a complete failure in personal relationships and a failure to love the fellow-men with whom we daily and actually come into contact. The outgoing love of the Christian is an outgoing love, not of humanity, but of men. The great and precious characteristic of Jesus is that again and again we find him giving all of himself to each individual person. It is quite possible to profess and even to feel a large benevolence for mankind, and at the same time to find the claims of some individual man nothing more than a nuisance. This outgoing mercy is a mercy which in fact goes out to my neighbour, as well as to mankind.

This could well be expressed by saying that this mercy is *actualised* outgoing love. It is not simply a sentiment; it is a life. It is not simply an emotion; it is action. The New Testament does not say: "God so loved the world", and stop there; it says, "God so loved the world that he gave his only begotten Son" (John 3. 16). This mercy is an outgoing love for man which actualises itself in action for individual men. Florence Allshorn said: "An ideal is not yours until it comes out of your finger-tips." This mercy lodges in the heart, but expresses itself in the hand. The desire to help becomes the deed of help, as it did in the case of God.

It remains to ask what this mercy, this *chesedh*, this outgoing love is. Love is a word with so many shades of meaning that we must try to define it more closely. T. H. Robinson says of *chesedh*: "It means a sympathetic appreciation of other persons; the power, not merely to concentrate blindly upon them, but to feel deliberately with them, to see life from their point of view." That is to say, *chesedh*, mercy, means the ability to get right into the other person's skin until we can see with his eyes, think with his mind, and feel with his heart. And that is to say that *chesedh*, mercy, comes from self-identification with other people. And herein lies the problem of mercy; most people are so concerned with their own thoughts and feelings and selves that they seldom or never even think of making this deliberate attempt to identify themselves with the mind and heart and life of their fellow-men. Mercy is far more than a wave of emotional pity; it is even more than help, as we think help to be needful. It comes from the willingness to forget self, and to make the deliberate and conscious effort to identify ourselves with other people. If we could and would make that self-identification with other people, certain great consequences would immediately follow.

It would make *tolerance* much easier. There is always a reason why a person thinks as he does think, and by entering into that person's mind and heart, and by seeing things with his eyes we could understand that reason, and tolerance would be much easier. John Wheatley was one of the famous Clyde-side members of Parliament. He spoke like a fire-brand and a revolutionary, and was regarded as a rebel. He was once talking to King George the Fifth. The king asked him why he was so violent an agitator. Wheatley quite simply told the king something of the slums of which he knew so much, and of the life that people had to live there, and of the spectre of unemployment, and the life of the working-man. When he had finished, the king said quietly: "If I had seen what you have seen, I too would be a revolutionary." The king had seen the world with Wheatley's eyes, and understood. Tolerance is only possible when we make the effort of self-identification with others.

It would make *forgiveness* much easier. There is always a reason why a person acts as he does. To know all is so often to be able to forgive all. It is easy to condemn a person or an action, when we are judging from the outside. No man has any real right to condemn another man until he has stood in the same position, and faced the same temptation, and come through the same battle. We cannot literally do that, but we can make the effort to identify ourselves with the other person, and when we do so there will come the understanding which leads to forgiveness.

It would make any *help* we give much more effective. There is a way of giving which we would never use, if we identified ourselves with the person to whom the help is given, for there is a way of giving which can do nothing but hurt and humiliate. On very many occasions our giving is decided by what we wish to give, or by what we think is good for the other person, and such giving may well not be the help that the other person stands in need of. If we made the effort of self-identification with others, then we would know both how to give and what to give.

So, then, this mercy, this *chesedh,* this outgoing love depends on a deliberate self-identification with our fellow-men. We have already seen that this mercy is a reflection and a reproduction in our attitude to our fellow-men of the attitude of God to all men. We, therefore, reach the final truth about this mercy. The supreme demonstration of this mercy is the Incarnation. In Jesus Christ God literally entered into our skin, seeing things with our eyes, thinking things with our minds, feeling things with our hearts. The Incarnation is God's complete self-identification with the sins, the sorrowings, and the sufferings of men. The supreme example of mercy is God's identification with men in Jesus Christ. The outgoing love of God was such that he made this supreme and sacrificial self-identification with man; and that is why God understands, forgives, and saves.

The Beatitude ends with the promise: "Blessed are the merciful, for they shall obtain mercy." Here is an inescapable principle laid down by Jesus. "With what judgment ye judge, ye shall be judged; and with what measure ye mete, it shall be measured to you again" (Matthew 7. 2). "If you forgive men their trespasses, your heavenly Father will also forgive you; but if ye forgive not men their tresspasses, neither will your Father forgive your trespasses" (Matthew 6. 14, 15). "He shall have judgment without mercy that hath showed no mercy" (James 2. 13). As a man judges, so he will be judged; as a man acted towards his fellow-men, so will God act upon him. It could not be otherwise. If this mercy, this outgoing love, this self-identification with others is the characteristic of the nature of God, then he who has practised it in his life will become more and more like God; and he who has made no attempt to practise it in his life will become ever and ever more distant from God. The practice of mercy is that which unites us with God; the failure in mercy is that which separates us from God. And so the ending of this Beatitude is promise and warning at one and the same time.

THE BLISS OF THE PURE IN HEART

Blessed are the pure in heart, for they shall see God
(MATTHEW 5. 8).

In this Beatitude, the Greek word that is used for *pure*
is a word with a very great width of meaning. It is for
that reason all the more necessary to study its meaning,
and to define the sense in which the Beatitude uses it.

The word is *katharos*. In classical and in secular Greek
it begins with a purely physical meaning, and can be used
of clothes which are clean in contrast with clothes which
are soiled and dirty. It has a whole series of meanings
which have to do with things which are without blemish,
without admixture, and without alloy. It is used of pure
water, and of wine and milk which are not adulterated
by water; of animals which are physically perfect, and
have no blemish; of grain which is winnowed from all
chaff, and of white bread which is made of the best of
flour; of silver and gold which have no alloy in them, but
which are sterling in their quality; of an army which has
been cleansed of all disaffected and inefficient soldiers
and which is a first-class fighting force, purged of every
undesirable element. It is used of blood, lineage, descent
which are absolutely pure, and of language which is

pure of all colloquialisms, errors of grammar and infelicities of style. It is used of a man who has been cleared of debt and who has been granted an absolute discharge from some duty which he has now fulfilled. It is used of a man who is ceremonially pure, and who is ceremonially fit to enter into the temple of his god. And, finally, it enters fully into the moral world and means free from pollution, free from defilement, and free from guilt. Very often it is used in epitaphs to pay tribute to one who all his or her life kept virtue unsullied and untarnished. The kindred word *katharsis* means *a purging draught,* which cleanses the body of all impurities. Here we clearly have a word with a very great history and a very wide variety of meanings.

But, as always when we wish to find the meaning of a word in the New Testament, we must look at the meaning of the word *katharos* in the Old Testament. In the Greek Old Testament *katharos* is very common, and occurs more than one hundred and fifty times. When we examine its use we find that it has two definite and distinct meanings. In the great majority of cases it describes *ceremonial* purity, the kind of foods and animals which may be eaten, the purity which comes from ceremonial washings and from all the observance of ritual laws, the kind of purity which is a matter of the observance of rules and regulations and which has little or no moral content at all. In Exodus *katharos* occurs thirty-seven times and in Leviticus it occurs thirty-four times and in no instance does it ever describe anything but this ceremonial and ritual purity. But *katharos* does, although not nearly so frequently, describe moral and

spiritual purity. It is used of Abraham in the sense of
integrity (Genesis 20. 5, 6), although the action of which
it is used was a very doubtful action. It is used to
describe blamelessness in face of a charge of misconduct
(Genesis 44. 10). In Job it is used in the sense of innocent,
upright, clear in the sight of God, and to describe the
prayer of a good man (Job 4. 7; 8. 6; 11. 4; 16. 17).
In the Psalms it is used of the pure heart and of the clean
heart (Psalm 24. 4; 51. 10). Isaiah uses it to mean clean
and pure from sin (Isaiah 1. 16). And it is the word
which is used in Habakkuk (1. 13) when it is said of
God that he is of purer eyes than to behold iniquity.

From all this one thing emerges quite clearly. In the
ancient world there were two conceptions of purity. One
conception regarded purity as a matter of ritual observances, as the continual obedience to a set of conventional
regulations and taboos, as entirely a ceremonial matter.
The other conception regarded purity as a matter of
life and conduct and a state of mind and heart.

First of all, let us look at the purity of ritual
observance. The very fact that *katharos* is so often used
in this sense in the Greek Old Testament is the proof of
how common and deep-seated and widespread this idea
of purity was. There were certain animals which were
clean and certain which were unclean (Leviticus 11). To
touch a dead body rendered a man unclean for seven
days (Numbers 19. 11-13). Before an orthodox Jew
sat at meat he washed his hands in a certain way, not
in the interests of hygiene, but in the interests of this
ritual and ceremonial purity. First of all he had to hold
each hand with the fingers pointing upwards, and pour

water over the hands until it reached at least up to the wrist; then he had to cleanse each palm by rubbing it with the fist of the other hand; then he had to hold the hands with the fingers pointing downwards, and pour water from the wrist so that it ran down the hand and off by the fingers. Not to do so was to be unclean, impure. On the Day of Atonement the High Priest had to wash his whole body in clean water five times, and his hands and feet ten times. Meticulously to observe these conventional rituals and ceremonies was held to make a man pure and to render him well-pleasing to God.

Another aspect of this comes out in the regulations governing elegibility for the priesthood. To be a priest a man must be a descendant of Aaron. Moral quality, spiritual insight, goodness, virtue, piety, holiness did not enter into the matter. With certain physical provisos, which we shall go on to see, if a man was a descendant of Aaron nothing could stop him being a priest; and if a man was not a descendant of Aaron all the saintliness and all the goodness in the world could not make him a priest. A man might be an arrogant sinner, an adulterer, an exploiter of his fellow-men; if he was a descendant of Aaron, he was a priest. A man might live with the grace of God irradiating him; if he was not a descendant of Aaron, he could not be a priest. The one proviso which limited this was the fact that the Law laid down one hundred and forty-two physical blemishes which disqualified a man from serving as a priest at the sacrifices in the Temple. Any physical blemish however small ruled a man out.

From this point of view purity had been completely

externalised; it was a matter of observing certain rituals and ceremonies; and the heart did not enter into it at all. So long as a man went through the conventional observances, he was pure.

That was what we might call the official and orthodox conception of purity in the time of Jesus; and Jesus completely contradicted it and dissociated himself from it in two words—Blessed are the pure *in heart*.

For Jesus purity was an inward thing, a thing of the heart and of the mind and of the attitude of the soul. On the orthodox Jewish point of view a man might have within his heart thoughts of arrogance and pride, thoughts of bitterness and hate, unclean thoughts and desires, but, so long as he observed the outward rituals correctly, he was pure. On Jesus' point of view, even if a man's outward actions were impeccably correct, and even if he observed every detail of the ceremonial law with meticulous devotion, he might still be utterly impure, because the thoughts of his heart were not right.

We need not be too quick to condemn the orthodox Jewish idea of purity as fantastically and obviously wrong. It is still possible to identify religion with outward observances. It is still possible to regard a man as a religious man because he observes all the outward conventions of religion—Church-going, Christian liberality, Bible-reading, respectability, pious language and the like—while in the eyes of Christ that man is utterly irreligious because the thoughts of his mind and the desires of his heart will not bear the scrutiny of God.

What, then, was this purity which Jesus demanded? It

is not surprising that by many this purity has been identified with sexual purity; but that is to narrow the meaning far too much. Origen (*Homily 73*, on John) says that it means "not only those who have been rid of fornication, but those who have been rid of all sins, for every sin leaves a stain upon the soul". We must go much deeper than that, for in his outward actions a man might strictly observe sexual purity and yet in his inmost thoughts transgress daily against it.

If we go back and re-examine the meanings of *katharos*, when it is used apart from ceremonial purity, we shall see that nearly all the other meanings of the word have one common element; they all describe something which has no tainting admixture of anything else. Unmixed milk or wine, unalloyed silver, winnowed corn are all *katharos*. They have no element in them to affect their purity. We can, therefore, say that " Blessed are the pure in heart " means " Blessed are those whose thoughts and motives are absolutely unmixed, and, therefore, absolutely pure." This Beatitude describes the bliss of the heart whose thoughts, motives, desires are completely unmixed, genuine, sincere.

When we realize what this Beatitude is saying it is the most demanding of all the Beatitudes. It necessitates the strictest and the most honest self-examination, and the end of that self-examination will infallibly be humiliation. Even an action which looks absolutely generous and even sacrificial may have in it some residue of self-satisfaction, of self-display, and of pride, even when we are scarcely conscious that it is so. In even the finest things there may be a lurking taint of pleasing self and courting the approval of men, even when we do not know it, until we rigorously search our own hearts. Even a man who to others seems a saint may, when he examines himself, find that he is the chief of sinners. There is no way to the purity that this Beatitude demands other than the death of self and the springing to life of Christ within the heart. Only the Christ who spoke this Beatitude can enable any man to enter into the bliss which this Beatitude promises.

The promise of this Beatitude is that the man who is pure in heart will see God. Even within the promise there is a warning. The very fact that the vision of God is promised to the pure in heart necessarily means that there are those to whom that vision cannot be given. It is a fact of life that what we see depends not only on what is in front of our eyes but also on what is within our minds and hearts. Knowledge makes a difference to seeing. The man who knows nothing of botany will see by the wayside a tangle of weeds and grasses and wild-flowers to none of which he can put a name; the skilled botanist will call each by name, and maybe will see something rare and unusual. The man with no know-ledge will go out into the night and see in the sky above him a mass of lights. He will not be able to name one of them, and will not be able to tell a star from a planet. The skilled astronomer will walk amongst the stars, calling them by name like his familiar friends; and by these same stars, which mean nothing to the man without knowledge, the navigator will bring back his ship to harbour. A doctor can tell things by looking at a patient as a layman never can; a scholar can see truth and beauty in a manuscript which is unintelligible to the man with no knowledge. What we know determines what we see. Experience makes a difference in seeing. That which leaves us quite unmoved when we are young, that which may even amuse a child, brings a stab to the heart and tears to the eyes, when the years have interpreted it and given it meaning. Moral character and the state of a man's mind make a difference to what he sees. A man can have a mind so depraved and unclean that he can see something to snigger about in anything, while to the pure all things are pure. It is so with us and God. Each day in life we are either fitting or unfitting ourselves to see God; we are either coming nearer to him or drifting further from him; we are making ourselves either more and more open or more and more shut to the vision of himself which he desires to send us.

The idea of seeing God is something which would immediately strike an answering chord in the heart and mind of people of the day of Jesus. The greatest privilege that a servant or a courtier could have was to have the right constantly to stand in the presence of the king, constantly to see his face, and to hear his wisdom. When the Queen of Sheba had heard all the wisdom of Solomon, she said: " Happy are thy men, happy these thy servants, who stand continually before thee, and hear thy wisdom " (I Kings 10. 8). The inmost group of the king's counsellors and friends were called " men of the king's presence " (II Kings 25. 19).

Even so, it was the great desire of men to see God as a king's friend saw their king. " I beseech thee," said

Moses, "shew me thy glory" (Exodus 33. 18). The greatest bliss that the Psalmist can imagine is to behold God's face in righteousness, and to be satisfied, when he awakes, with the likeness of God (Psalm 17. 15). It is his hope that because of his integrity God sets him before his face for ever (Psalm 41. 12). His great desire is to see the power and the glory of God as in the past he has seen them in the sanctuary of God (Psalm 63. 2). The upright will dwell in the presence of God (Psalm 140. 13). Bliss is to be for ever in the presence of God.

There are times when in Scripture it is said that it is impossible for any man to see God. It is God's answer to Moses: "There shall no man see me and live" (Exodus 33. 20). When Manoah discovered who his heavenly visitor had been, he said in terror to his wife: "We shall surely die because we have seen God" (Judges 13. 22). But to see God is not literally to see God with the physical eye; that is not possible. "No man hath seen God at any time" (John 1. 18). To see God means two things.

It means to enter into fullness of knowledge of God. It is what Paul meant when he said: "Now we see through a glass, darkly; but then face to face: now I know in part; but then shall I know even as also I am known" (I Corinthians 13. 12). It means to have done with guessing and groping and to see and to know the truth.

It means to enter into the intimate fellowship of love. Love's highest joy is to be in the presence of the loved one. Mrs. A. R. Cousin wrote the lines, paraphrasing the thoughts of Samuel Rutherford:

I shall sleep sound in Jesus,
    Fill'd with His likeness rise,
To live and to adore Him,
    To see Him with these eyes.

    . . . .

The Bride eyes not her garment,
    But her dear Bridegroom's face;
I will not gaze at glory,
    But on my King of grace—
Not at the crown He gifteth,
    But on His nail-pierced hand;
The *Lamb* is all the glory
    Of Immanuel's land.

The man whose heart has been cleansed in Jesus and by the Spirit of God, the man whose motives, thoughts, emotions, desires are absolutely unmixed, will be given nothing less than the vision of God. The beginning of the fulfilment of this promise will be even here in time, but the completing of it will need all eternity. Even here we have in Jesus Christ a new and living way into the presence of God, but hereafter the rending veil will reveal to us God as he is, if we have kept ourselves pure in his grace, and the search for knowledge will find its answer, and the desire of love will find its satisfaction in the presence of God.

THE BLISS OF THE
BREAKER-DOWN OF BARRIERS

Blessed are the peacemakers, for they shall be called the children of God (MATTHEW 5. 9).

It may well be that time's changes in the meaning of words have narrowed for us the meaning of this Beatitude. For us peace is largely a negative word; it tends to describe mainly the absence or the cessation of war and trouble. Even in a situation in which a land was devastated, in which cities were in ruins, and in which men, women and children were starving, if war came to an end, we would likely say that peace had returned. But for a Jew peace had a far wider meaning than that. The Greek word for peace is *eirene,* which translates the Hebrew word *shalom. Shalom* has two main meanings. It describes perfect welfare, serenity, prosperity and happiness. The eastern greeting is *Salaam,* and that greeting does not only wish a man freedom from trouble; it wishes him everything which makes for his contentment and his good. For the Jew peace is a condition of perfect and complete positive well-being. Second, *shalom* describes right personal relationships; it describes intimacy, fellowship, uninterrupted goodwill between man and man. It can easily be seen that peace does not describe only the absence of war and strife; peace describes happiness and well-being of life, and perfection of human relationships. When the Psalmist prays that peace should be within the walls of Jerusalem (Psalm 122. 7, 8), he is praying that every good blessing should descend upon the city and upon its citizens.

It would be true to say that the New Testament is the book of this peace. In it the word *peace, eirene,* occurs eighty-eight times, and it occurs in every book. One of the great characteristics of the New Testament letters is that they begin and end with a prayer for peace for those who are to read and to listen to them. Paul begins every one of his letters with the prayer that grace and peace may be on the people to whom he writes, and often the New Testament letters end with some such phrase as, "Peace be to you all." When Jesus was leaving his disciples, as John tells the story, he said to them: "Peace I leave with you, my peace I give unto you" (John 14. 27). J. S. Stewart has called that the last will and testament of Jesus. Of worldly goods and possessions Jesus had nothing to leave, but he left to men his peace.

We must mark one all-important fact in this Beatitude —the people to whom the blessing is promised. The people who are blessed are not the peace-*lovers* but the peace-*makers*. It can happen that a man is a peaceful man and a peace-lover, and is yet not a peace-maker. A man may know that there is something wrong in some situation, in his family, in his Church, in some group of which he is a member; he may know that something ought to be done to rectify the situation; but he may also know that any step taken to mend the situation may well involve difficulty and trouble and problems which it will not be pleasant to face. In such a situation a man may well decide to do and say nothing, as he will put it, "for peace's sake". He will allow the situation to continue and the whole matter to drift uneasily on, because his love of a certain kind of peace makes him evade all trouble. Such a man may be called a peaceable man and a peace-lover; but he is certainly not a peace-maker; he is rather in the end a trouble-maker; for the longer any situation is allowed to continue the more serious its consequences and the harder its cure. The man who is blessed is the man who is prepared to face difficulty, unpleasantness, unpopularity, trouble in order to *make* peace. The peace of which this Beatitude speaks is not the spurious peace which comes from evading the issue; it is the peace which comes from facing the issue, and from being prepared to give everything in toil and in sacrifice which the situation demands. In his translation Luther translates the Greek by the word "peaceable", but in the margin he adds and explains this by saying that it means "those who make and preserve peace among one another; and they are more than peaceable."

Let us then look at the meaning of this peace whose makers are blessed.

Peace, *shalom,* as we have seen, means welfare and well-being at their best and at their highest. Therefore, this Beatitude means that all those who do anything to increase the well-being and the welfare of the world are blessed. The work of social reformation is work for God. Those whose zeal and toil produce houses which are fit to live in and conditions which are fit to work in are in the realest sense servants of God. Those who find new ways of conquering pain and healing the sick, those who toil that the hungry may be fed and that the aged may be tended are in the realest sense doing the work of God. Those who do anything to make life in the world fuller and happier and easier for others are truly serving God. If all men are the children of God, then their heavenly Father cares how they live, how they work, how they are fed and clothed, how they are treated in weakness, in want, in age and in pain. The man with a passion for the welfare of his fellow-men is serving God in serving men, and is therefore blessed.

We get even nearer to the meaning of this Beatitude when we take peace, *shalom,* in its other meaning of *right relationships.* The Jewish Rabbis taught that those who honour father and mother, those who do good, and those who make peace between people reap good fruits alike in this life and the life to come. In every man's life there are three relationships; and in each case it is of the greatest importance that the relationship should be right.

There is a man's *relationship to himself,* and blessed, indeed, is the man who has succeeded in coming to a right relationship with himself. This is the sense in which the early fathers of the Church frequently took this Beatitude. Clement of Alexandria took it to be a blessing on " those who have stilled the incredible battle which goes on in their own souls ". Augustine took it to be a blessing on those " who have composed and subjected to reason all the motions of their minds, and who have tamed their carnal desires ".

It is a fact of experience that every man is at least to some extent a split personality. It was the Jewish belief that in every man there were two natures, the good nature which drew him up, and the evil nature which dragged him down. It was as if a good angel stood at his right hand beckoning him to goodness, and an evil angel stood at his left hand beckoning him to evil. Life has been described as "an endless war of contrarieties". This is the struggle of which Paul wrote so movingly in the seventh chapter of Romans. "The good that I would, I do not; but the evil which I would not, I do" (Romans 7. 19). There was a war in his members between two laws, the one urging him to goodness, the other enticing him to sin. This was the picture which Plato drew of human nature. He pictured the soul as a charioteer. Yoked to the chariot there are two horses. The one horse is wild and untamed; the other is gentle and under control. The name of the first horse is passion, and the name of the second horse is reason; and somehow the soul has to control them and to make them run in double harness. A. E. Housman in one of his verses vividly expresses the universal human experience:

> More than I, if truth were told,
> Have stood and sweated hot and cold,
> While through their veins, like ice and fire,
> Fear contended with desire.

Robert Burns was well aware of the wreckage which he so often made of life. "My life," he said, "reminded me of a ruined temple; what strength, what proportion in some parts, what unsightly gaps, what ruin in others."

Studdert Kennedy describes the feelings of a soldier in
the first world war. The public tried to treat him as
a hero; the padre insisted on treating him as a hell-
deserving sinner.

> Our padre says I'm a sinner,
> And John Bull says I'm a saint,
> And they're both of them bound to be liars,
> For I'm neither of them, I ain't.
> I'm a man, and a man's a mixture,
> Right down from his very birth,
> For part of him comes from heaven,
> And part of him comes from earth.
> There's nothing in him that's perfect;
> There's nothing that's all complete.
> He's nobbut a great beginning
> From his head to the soles of his feet.

Every man well knows that he is a mixture. We know
that we are capable at one time of an almost saintly
goodness, and at another time of an almost devilish evil.
We know that at one time we are capable of an almost
sacrificial kindness, and at another of an almost heartless
callousness. We know that sometimes the vision of goodness fills our horizon, and that other times the unclean
and evil desire has us at its mercy. We are part ape
and part angel.

There is clearly neither happiness or security in a
life like that. There is continuous tension, continuous
inner debate. A man is a walking civil war, never
knowing which side within him will win the victory.
Man as he is is a disintegrating personality and stands in
need of integration. Clearly such integration can only

come when some other force and power take possession of a man; something from outside him has to come in and take control; and that can only happen when a man can say what Paul said: "I live, yet not I, but Christ liveth in me" (Galatians 2. 20). Blessed indeed is the man who is at peace with himself, the man in whom the contradictions are obliterated, the man whose inner battle has been stilled in the control of Christ. Every man must long for peace in the inner warfare of his own personality and his own soul; and Jesus Christ is the only person who can make that peace.

There is a man's *relationship to his fellow-men*. Blessed is he who produces right relationships between man and man. There is little doubt that it is in this sense that a Jew would have taken this Beatitude, for, as we have already seen, to a Jew there were few higher achievements of this world than that of creating right relationships between men; and nothing is more necessary in this world than the creation of such relationships.

We live in a divided world with its iron curtains, its lines of demarcation, its divisions between race and race, nation and nation, and man and man. The strange Old Testament story regards this divided world as the curse of God upon man for man's overweening pride (Genesis 11. 1-9). It tells how men in their pride united to attempt to build a tower which would reach to heaven, and how God in punishment confounded and confused their languages so that they should be divided for ever after.

In the ancient world there was the division between Gentile and Jew. To this day if the son or daughter of a strictly orthodox Jewish family marries a Gentile, the family will carry out his funeral, for he is as one who is dead. In the ordinary form of morning prayer a Jew thanks God that God did not make him a Gentile, a slave or a woman. Even before God Jew and Gentile were separated. In the Temple in Jerusalem there were a series of Courts leading into the Holy Place. There was the Court of the Gentiles, the Court of the Women, the Court of the Israelites, and the Court of the Priests. Beyond the outer Court of the Gentiles the Gentile could not go. Between it and the Court of the Women there was a balustrade called the *Chel*. Inset at intervals along this balustrade there were stone tablets with the inscription on them: "No person of another race is to enter within the balustrade and embankment round the sacred place. Whoever is caught so doing will be answerable for his own death, which will follow." For the Gentile to seek the nearer presence of the God of the Jews was death.

In the Greek world there was what the Greeks called a "natural" division between Greek and barbarian, and by the word "natural" the Greek meant a barrier and a difference which was in the very course of nature, in the very structure of the world, something which must continue to be as long as the world should be. As Plato saw it, the barbarians were the natural enemies of the Greeks. Isocrates held that the greatness of Homer's poetry lay in the fact that it told of the wars of the Greeks against the barbarians, and held that Homer must always hold his place in the education of the young so that boys in every age might learn and imitate that ancient hatred. In the Greek Mystery Religions murderers and barbarians were classed together as being shut out; and all through this it must be remembered that a barbarian to the Greek was simply one who did not speak Greek.

In the modern world the divisions continue. There seems to be in the human mind an ineradicable suspicion of the stranger, so the suspicion of nation against nation continues. That suspicion is exacerbated when nations follow different philosophies of life, or when men are of different colours.

It is quite clear that a world like that cannot be other than a world which is both unhappy and unsafe. It is a world in which men must always be on guard, in which men must bend resources which could well have been devoted to better things to the purposes either of attack or self-defence, a world which may at any time erupt into a volcano of war and bloodshed. Aggrey of Africa did a great work as Principal of Achimoto College in West Africa. He died all too young, but he wrote his memory in the badge which he devised for the College. The badge was part of the keyboard of a piano with black and white notes. The symbolism is that some kind of music can no doubt be produced by using the white notes alone, or by using the black notes alone; but the best music can only be produced when black and white notes are used together in harmony. The danger of division is clear, and all man's troubled history is a demonstration of it; the desirability of unity is equally clear, as all men's prayers and visions combine to show. But the problem is where that unity is to find its source and its dynamic. The ancient Stoics believed that all men were born to be united, because that which gave all men life was that a spark of God had taken up its dwelling-place within their bodies. Men were men because they shared the common life of God, and, therefore, men should share all life together. Zeno, the founder of Stoicism, regarded the perfect state as a state which would include all men. In it a man would no longer say, " I am a citizen of Athens," but, " I am a citizen of the world." In the ideal state there would be no such thing as a lawcourt, for men would never dispute with one another. T. H. Robinson, commenting on this Beatitude says : " The ideal of God for human society is a spiritual condition in which jealousy, rivalry and hostility have disappeared, and a universal harmony prevails. He who is most worthy of congratulation for his true success in this difficult and complicated world of men and women is he who most perfectly succeeds in producing and upholding this harmony."

In no other power can this unity be found than in the power of Jesus Christ. There is abundant evidence that Jesus Christ can produce this unity. Bishop Lesslie Newbiggin tells of an experience in his diocese in India. When the United Church of South India came into being, and when he became one of its bishops, he made an introductory tour of his diocese. At each village the Christian community came out to meet its bishop. In one village the Christians were led by an extraordinary figure, clad in very aged R.A.F. equipment, and carrying a stainless steel baton. With this baton he controlled, as it were, his congregation. At a sign from him they knelt, and at another sign they rose. Bishop Newbiggin was staying with him when his story came out. His name was Sundaram. At the beginning of the second world war he was preaching the gospel in Burma. He was captured in the advance of the Japanese armies. He was taken to a guard-post. Everything he possessed was taken from him and he was bound and thrown into a corner. A Japanese officer came in. He went to the table where Sundaram's scanty belongings lay. He picked up the Tamil Bible. He knew no word of Tamil but he recognised it as a Bible. He held up his hand and traced on the palm the sign of the Cross and looked questioningly at Sundaram. Sundaram knew no word of Japanese, but he knew that the officer was asking if he was a Christian, and he nodded. The officer walked across to him, stood in front of him with his arms stretched out in the form of the Cross, cut his bonds, gave him back his belongings, and pointed to the door, bidding him to go. And, before Sundaram went out to freedom, the Japanese officer handed him as a token and memento his officer's staff; and that officer's staff was the stainless steel baton with which Sundaram directed his Indian congregation. Here were two men who knew not a word of each other's language, two men from nations which were at war, two men between whom there stretched a gulf which was humanly speaking beyond bridging—and Christ bridged that gulf. Jesus Christ reached out across the divisions and in Christ brought two men together again.

The phrase "Christ the Hope of the World" was never truer than it is to-day. If it were only possible that the Christian missionary might take the place of the

invading army the peace of right relationships might yet
come true in our time.

But the world in which we live has its divisions not
only between nation and nation, but also between
individual and individual. It is so often true that the
human heart is the home of bitterness and of the
unforgiving spirit. No one knew better than Jesus the
tragedy of the jealousies and the envies and the bitter-
nesses which separate man and man, for they invaded
even the apostolic company. On the way to Jerusalem
they were arguing among themselves about who should
be greatest (Mark 9. 34). James and John came with their
ambitious request for the principal places in the
kingdom, and there was trouble among the Twelve
(Mark 10. 35-45). Even at the Last Supper within the
shadow of the Cross the Twelve were arguing about
pre-eminence and about the first place (Luke 22. 24).
Again, it is only Jesus Christ who can in himself create
the right relationship between man and man. Bryan
Greene talks of an incident in one of his American
campaigns. At the end of the campaign he gathered
a number of those who had shared in the campaign and
who had found Christ, and asked them to state in one
brief sentence without elaboration what the campaign
had done for them and meant to them. There was a
negro girl there. She had no difficulty in being brief, for
she had no ability in words. She rose and she said:
"Through this campaign I found Jesus Christ, and he
made me able to forgive the man who murdered my
father." *He made me able to forgive.* It is only when
men enter into the right relationship with Jesus Christ

that they can enter into the right relationship with each other.

Herein is part of the task of the Christian. The Christian must labour to produce right relationships between man and man. In any society, in the private society of a home, and in the public society of an institution or a Church, there are those who are disruptive influences and there are those who are reconciling influences. There are those who sow strife and there are those who sow peace. It must always be remembered that Christian reconciliation has a Godward and a manward look. It means the reconciliation of men to God and of men to each other; and there are few who are more blessed than those who produce and who maintain and who restore right relationships between man and man.

Man has a third relationship; he has a *relationship with God*. Man's relationship may be simply a consciousness of immense difference and infinite distance. It may be a relationship of fear and alienation in which a man tries to hide from God, as Adam did in the old story (Genesis 3. 8). It may be a relationship of enmity and hostility. Swinburne could speak of " the supreme evil— God ". It may be a relationship of complete indifference in which a man lives as if God did not exist. But it is easy to see the difference it must make to any man to see in the creator, the sustainer and the governor of the universe one in whose heart there is only love. Here again only Jesus Christ can produce that relationship. Whatever else is true of Jesus, this is certainly true, that in Jesus Christ we see perfectly displayed the attitude of

God to men; and when we realize that in Jesus Christ we see the Father (John 14. 9), that God is like Jesus, then there is born between us and God the new relationship in which, instead of avoiding his presence, we seek it, in which, instead of fleeing from him, we seek him, in which we find ourselves at home in the presence of God.

Blessed, indeed, is the man who breaks down the barriers between nation and nation, between man and man, and between man and God. Happy is the man whose life-work is the production of right relationships in ever sphere of life; and such relationships can only enrich life when a man's own relationship to Jesus Christ is right.

After the affirmation of the Beatitude there comes the promise. The peacemakers shall be called the children of God. The phrase " shall be called " is a Hebrew way of saying " shall be acknowledged to be ", or, " shall receive the status of ", or, " shall be owned and regarded as ". The peacemakers will enter into the honour of being the children of God. Further, the translation *children of God* is not quite accurate. It ought to be *sons of God,* and this in Hebrew has a special meaning. Hebrew is deficient in adjectives; there is, for instance, no adjective in the twenty-third psalm. To make up for this deficiency Hebrew uses the phrase *son of* plus some virtue or quality instead of an adjective. Barnabas, for instance, is the son of consolation; that is, he is a consoling and a comforting man. James and John are the sons of thunder; that is, they are thunderous and stormy characters. A man may be called a son of peace; that is, he is a peaceful and well-disposed man. So then the

phrase " sons of God " means God-like. The translation
of this Beatitude might well read: " Blessed are those
who produce right relationships in every sphere of life,
for they are doing a God-like work."

Repeatedly in the New Testament God is called the
God of peace (Romans 15. 13; 16. 20; Philippians 4. 9;
II Corinthians 13. 11; I Timothy 5. 23; Hebrews
13. 20, 21). God is the great establisher of right
relationships; he gave his Son to establish and restore
the right relationship between Himself and men; and,
therefore, those who labour, toil and pray to bring right
relationships between man and man and between man
and God and between man and his own storm-tossed
and divided heart can fitly be said to be God-like, and
can fitly be said to be doing a God-like work. No
man is more nearly kin to God than the man whose
life is spent bringing peace among men, and no man's
bliss is greater.

THE BLISS OF THE MARTYR'S PAIN

Blessed are they which are persecuted for righteousness'
sake, for theirs is the kingdom of heaven.

Blessed are ye, when men shall revile you, and
persecute you, and shall say all manner of evil against
you falsely, for my sake.

Rejoice, and be exceeding glad, for great is your
reward in heaven; for so persecuted they the prophets
which were before you. (MATTHEW 5. 10-12).

One of the most illuminating and significant facts about
the language of the early Church is that before the end
of the first century the word for *witness* and the word
for *martyr* had become the same Greek word. The
word is *martus;* its original meaning in ordinary Greek
is *witness;* but this is the word which came also to mean
martyr, because in that time the man who was a witness
had every chance of being a martyr too. There are,
indeed, times when we do not know which of the two
meanings of this Greek word the New Testament writers
would have had us to choose in translation. In the letter
to Smyrna John speaks of " Antipas my faithful *martus* "
(Revelation 2. 13); and we can equally well say that
Antipas was the faithful *witness* and the faithful *martyr*

of Christ, because for him, as for so many in these killing times, the one meaning implied the other. This is the Beatitude which tells of the bliss of the martyr's pain.

We must begin by thinking of the inevitability of persecution. There was in Jesus an almost startling honesty; no one could ever say that he had been induced to follow Jesus on false pretences; Jesus told his followers what they might expect, and he left them in no doubt that they must suffer for his name. To follow him necessarily involved the taking up of a cross (Matthew 16. 24). He had no doubt that his men would be brought before the magistrates, that they would be scourged in the Synagogues, and that they would be hated by all men because of their fidelity to him (Matthew 10. 16-22; Mark 13. 9; Luke 21. 17). The day would come when those who killed a Christian would think that they were rendering service to God (John 16. 2). They were not of the world as Jesus had not been of the world; and as the world had hated him, so it would necessarily hate them (John 15. 18, 19; 17. 14). The *world* in the Johannine sense of the term has been defined as " human nature organising itself without God ", and human nature apart from God must be in opposition to human nature which has taken God as the centre of existence. The day was to come when Peter, surely remembering this Beatitude, was to tell his people, who were going through it, that bliss was theirs, if they suffered, as Christ suffered, for righteousness' sake (I Peter 3. 14), and if they were reproached for the name of Christ (I Peter 4. 14). Jesus left his

followers in no doubt of the cost of following him, and
of the cross that loyalty to him involved.

What, then, were the reasons which from the heathen
point of view made persecution inevitable?

There was the simple but basic fact that the Christians
were different; and men always regard with suspicion
that which is different. As far as the public is concerned,
conformity is the way to a trouble-free life, and the
Christians were inevitably non-conformists. "We have
the reputation," said Tertullian, "of living aloof from
crowds" (*Apology* 31). The Christians, as the heathen
saw them, were people who "skulk in corners and shun
the light of day, silent in public, but full of talk in their
holes and corners", "people who separate themselves
from the rest of mankind" (Minucius Felix, *Octavius* 8).

The difference of the Christian came out in all kinds
of ways, and to this essential difference we will later
return. The Christians had a completely different moral
standard. Chastity was a new virtue, and a new demand.
The Christian had perforce to abandon all social life.
Every heathen meal began with a libation and a prayer
to the pagan gods; in that a Christian could not share.
Most heathen feasts and social parties were held in the
precincts of a temple, after sacrifice had been made, and
the invitation was usually the invitation to dine "at the
table" of some god. To such a feast a Christian could not
go. Inevitably the Christian seemed rude, boorish and
discourteous when he refused the invitation to some social
occasion. Even in the ordinary working life of the time
the Christian was a problem. True, the Christian did

not argue in favour of the emancipation of slaves, but he treated a slave as a brother, as, indeed, he believed him to be. Callistus, the third bishop of Rome, was a slave; he bitterly exacerbated heathen feeling by allowing marriage between high-born girls and freedmen who had been slaves, if both were Christian, and a marriage such as that was in the eyes of the Roman law quite illegal and no marriage at all. Roman civilisation was built on slavery and the Christians seemed to be undermining its very foundations. If a Christian was going to be strictly consistent and rigorous in his witness almost any trade was a danger. Clearly he could not be a gladiator or an actor; but even a mason might be involved in building the walls of a heathen temple, a tailor in making robes for a heathen priest, an incense-maker in making incense for the heathen sacrifices. Tertullian the rigorist even forbade a Christian to be a school teacher, because such teaching involved using as text-books the books which told the ancient stories of the gods, and observing the religious festivals of the pagan year. The Christian was almost bound to divorce himself from even the social and economic life of his time, and no man who divorces himself from his fellow-men in order to be better than his fellow-men can hope to be popular. The Christians were hated as men who seemed to wish to stand aloof from their fellow-men, and as men whose customs and way of life seemed likely to disrupt the social set-up of life.

At least some of the persecution directed against the Christians was connected with the Jews. The Jewish connection with persecution was twofold. First, since the early Christians at the beginning of the Church were almost all Jews, and since Christianity took its rise in Palestine, and since Jesus himself was a Jew, in its earliest days Christianity and Judaism were inextricably confounded in the heathen mind. To the heathen Christianity seemed to be a Jewish sect. Anti-semitism is no new thing, and in the ancient world the Jews were bitterly hated. All kinds of slanders about the Jews were prevalent. It was said that in the Holy of Holies there was an ass's head, because in the wilderness the Jews had been led by wild asses to water when they were perishing of thirst. Plutarch did not accept this story, but he suggested that the god of the Jews was the pig, because swine's flesh was sacred to them (Tacitus, *Histories* 5. 2-5; Plutarch, *Symposium* 4. 5; Juvenal, *Satires* 14. 96-106). The Jewish habit of observing the Sabbath gained them a reputation for idleness and laziness. " O Marcomanni, O Quadi, O Sarmatians," said Marcus Aurelius, " at last I have discovered a people more lazy than you " (*Ammianus Marcellinus* 22. 5). Worse than that, the rumour ran in Alexandria that once a year the Jews sacrificed a Gentile to their gods. It is true that the Jews were specially protected by the Romans, because, being the world's financiers and traders then as now, they were valuable members of the state. But every now and then there were popular bursts of violence against them, and they were always regarded with extreme dislike. Inevitably the Christians shared in this hatred, and inevitably the Christians were involved in the persecution which fell on the Jews at frequent intervals. Second, it is a fact that the Jews were behind at least some of the persecutions which fell upon the Christians. The Jews had access to the ear of those who were in authority. Their place in the business and commercial life of the world brought them into contact with the government and with the highest in the land. Very naturally they made every effort to dissociate themselves from the Christians and to make it clear that they had no connection with them; and often they used their influence to persuade the authorities to take action against the Christians. Around the Synagogue there gathered many Gentiles who were attracted by the Jewish belief in one God, and by the Jewish moral and ethical code, even if they were not prepared to accept circumcision and the whole Jewish law. In particular the moral teaching of Judaism was attractive to women. Many of the women who came to worship in the Synagogues were the wives of high government officials, and the Jews, as in Antioch (Acts 13. 50), did not hesitate to exert an influence against Christianity by persuading these women to persuade their husbands to put the law into action against the Christians. "The Synagogues," said Tertullian, "are the sources of persecution" (*Scorpiace* 10). Persecution came upon the Christians because in the popular mind they were confused with the Jews, and because the Jews used their widespread influence to foment persecution against them.

The Christians were accused of atheism. There were many among the heathen who could not understand an imageless worship, and for whom monotheism had no attraction. Even more serious, the Christians were accused of insulting the gods of the state. It is true that there was very little reality in the worship of the ancient gods by the time Christianity came to this world; but the worship of these old gods was still the state worship; it was part of a good citizen's duty to observe that worship: and the feeling was that, if that worship was not observed, the ancient gods took their revenge by sending disasters upon the state. The worship of the gods might be a convention, but it was a convention which for safety's sake had to be observed. So Tertullian writes: " If the Tiber floods the city, or if the Nile refuses to rise, or if the sky withholds its rain, if there is an earthquake, a famine, a pestilence, at once the cry is raised: ' The Christians to the lions.' " (Tertullian, *Apology* 40). Augustine tells us that in North Africa it has become a proverb, " If there is no rain, blame the Christians " (Augustine, *The City of God* 2. 3), and his greatest work *The City of God* is indeed designed to show that the sack of Rome in A.D. 410 was not due to the anger of the insulted and abandoned gods. It was easy and convenient to make the Christians the scapegoats for any disaster in the world.

One of the undeniable effects of Christianity was that it in fact did often make a division in the family. In that sense it was poignantly true that Christianity came not with peace but with a sword. An agonising situation was bound to arise when a son or a daughter became a Christian in defiance of the family, or when a husband and wife were divided by this new religion. It was literally true that Christianity could set a man at variance with his nearest and dearest, and that a man's foes could be those of this own household (Matthew 10. 34-37).

A Christian has to be prepared to love Christ more than he loved those who upon earth were closest to him. It was inevitable that the Christians should incur the charge of " tampering with family relationships ". Inevitably the heathen would hate this religion which disrupted their homes.

Even if the home was not disrupted, there were serious problems. A wife might become a Christian and a husband remain a pagan, and the two might still live together. But Tertullian tells us of the heathen husband who resented the fact that his wife " in order to visit the brethren goes from street to street to other men's houses, especially those of the poor. . . . He will not allow her to be present at all night long meetings and paschal solemnities. . . . He will not allow her to creep into prison to kiss a martyr's chains, or even to exchange the kiss of peace with one of the brethren " (Tertullian, *To his Wife* 2. 4. 5). One cannot but feel a certain amount of sympathy for the husband. It is clear that Christianity must often have produced a very difficult situation in many a home, and must in many cases have been heartily hated.

High on the list of things which brought hatred upon the Christians were the slanders which were disseminated about them, and which, once they were started, could not be halted. Mommsen writes: " The conviction that the Christian conventicles were orgies of lewdness, and receptacles of every crime, got hold on the popular mind with all the terrible vehemence of an aversion that resists all arguments and heeds not refutation." These slanders were accentuated by the secrecy of the Christian services, and especially by the fact that all who were not Christians were barred rigorously from the Sacrament. Secrecy always begets suspicion. The main slanders were three. The Christians were charged with cannibalism, a charge which came from the words of the Sacrament which speak of eating and drinking the body and the blood of Christ. They were charged with gross immorality, a charge which came from the fact that the Christian meeting was called the Agapé, the Love Feast, and from the custom of the kiss of peace, which the brethren gave to one another, and which, indeed, in the end became so liable to abuse that it was almost completely abandoned. It was alleged that the Christians killed and ate a child at their sacred meals. This may have been a reckless and a malicious allegation based on the fact that Christians were seen to carry children to the Christian meeting for baptism. It is not difficult to see how such charges could arise, and it is easy to see how the enemies of Christianity could use them as ammunition against the Christians, even if they knew them to be false, for there would be many who were more than willing to believe the worst.

We have not even yet come to the supreme cause of persecution. The supreme cause of persecution was the head-on clash between Christianity and Cæsar worship. Cæsar worship means the worship of the Roman Emperor as a god. Cæsar worship had a long history and a long development. In the great days of the Empire and of the Republic before it, the provincials did not resent the Roman sway; in many cases they welcomed it with wondering and heartfelt gratitude. There were even cases of kings voluntarily and of their own free will handing over and bequeathing their kingdoms to Rome. Rome brought to the world the *pax Romana,* the Roman peace. When the Romans took over the government of a country, impartial Roman justice arrived, and men were freed from the capricious government of unpredictable and often savage and bloodthirsty tyrants. When Roman administration came, the roads were cleared of brigands and the seas of pirates, and a new security entered into life. As E. J. Goodspeed put it: "The provincial, under Roman sway, found himself in a position to conduct his business, provide for his family, send his letters, and make his journeys in security, thanks to the strong hand of Rome." The result of this was a deep and heartfelt gratitude to the spirit of Rome. It was an easy step for the spirit of Rome to become the goddess Roma, and by the second century B.C. there were many temples in Asia Minor to the goddess Roma. But the human mind and heart characteristically need a symbol; it was a further easy step to see the goddess Roma and the spirit of Rome incarnated in the Emperor. He embodied Rome; he was Rome; in him the spirit of Rome resided and had its earthly dwelling. The first temple actually built to the godhead of the Emperor was built in Pergamum in 29 B.C.

So far the worship of Rome and of the Emperor was a quite spontaneous growth, not in any way imposed upon the people. At first the Emporors were very hesitant about this. Claudius refused to have temples erected to him because, as he said, he did not wish to be offensive to his fellow-men. But slowly an idea began to dawn and form in the official mind. The problem of the Roman Empire was the problem of unification. The Empire stretched from the river Euphrates and beyond it to Britain and the shores of the Irish sea. It stretched from Germany to North Africa, from Spain to Egypt. Here were all kinds of peoples, and languages, and faiths, and traditions. How could they be welded into a unity? How could there be brought into their lives the consciousness of being one empire? There is no unifying force like the force of a common religion; and Cæsar worship lay ready to hand. None of the local and ancestral faiths had any hope of ever becoming universal, but Rome was universal. The result was, as W. M. Ramsay says, that Cæsar worship became " the keystone " of imperial policy. It was deliberately universalised; it was deliberately organised in every province in the Empire. Everywhere temples to the godhead of the Emperor were erected. It was precisely the cost of the administration of Caesar worship in the Roman temple in the city which is now Colchester that provided the tragic and disastrous revolt of Boadicea in Britain in A.D. 61

There was another step to be taken—and it was taken. Cæsar worship was made universal—and it was made compulsory for every race and nation within the Empire with the single exception of the Jews. On a certain day in the year every Roman citizen had to come to the Temple of Cæsar and had to burn a pinch of incense there, and say: "Cæsar is Lord." When he had done that, he was given a certificate to certify that he had done so, and that certificate he had to get.

We must note one thing. The Romans were the reverse of intolerant; they were the most tolerant masters the world has ever seen. After a man had burned his pinch of incense and had acknowledged Cæsar as Lord, he could go away and worship any god he liked, so long as the worship did not affect public decency and public order. It can be seen at once that Cæsar worship was first and foremost a test of political loyalty; it was a test of whether or not a man was a good citizen; and, if a man refused to carry out the ceremony of acknowledging Cæsar, he was automatically branded as a traitor and a revolutionary and a disloyal and disaffected citizen.

It was here that Christianity and Cæsar worship met in head-on collision. The one thing which no Christian would ever say was: "Cæsar is Lord." For the Christian Jesus Christ and Jesus Christ alone was Lord. To the Roman the Christian seemed utterly intolerant and insanely stubborn; worse, he seemed a self-admittedly disloyal citizen. Had the Christians been willing to burn that pinch of incense and to say formally, "Cæsar is Lord," they could have gone on worshipping Christ to their heart's content; but the Christians would not compromise. Rome regarded them as a band of potential revolutionaries threatening the very being of the Empire; and Rome struck and struck again.

It was not that persecution was constant and consistent. For long periods the Christians were left in peace. But like a sword of Damocles persecution was always poised above them. It only took a malicious informer, a popular demand, a governor determined to carry out the letter of the law, and the storm would burst. The Christian as a Christian was legally an outlaw. "Public hatred," says Tertullian, "asks but one thing, and that not investigating into the crimes charged, but simply the confession of the Christian name" (Tertullian, *Apology* 2).

So we see that Jewish malevolence, popular slander and dislike, and political principles all converged to make the persecution of the Christians inevitable. A Christian, as a Christian, was regarded as the enemy of the state, as a public enemy, an outlaw.

When we look at the experiences of the persecuted, we see even more vividly the amazing paradox which this Beatitude contains when it speaks of the bliss of the martyr's pain. The persecution of the Christians took more than one form. At its mildest it would involve social ostracism; the Christian would inevitably become an outsider, to whom the doors once open would now be shut. The Christian, as we have seen, would have to face a constant campaign of slander. The First Epistle of Peter more than once speaks of those who speak evil against the Christians (I Peter 2. 12; 3. 16). The Christian day by day lived in a society in which the most slanderous tales were whispered, and even shouted from the housetops, against him. There were times when this pagan suspicion and dislike erupted in an outbreak of looting and destruction and mob violence. The Letter to the Hebrews tells how the Christians have uncomplainingly accepted the spoiling of their goods (Hebrews 10. 34). But it is when we see the sadistic and savage ingenuity of the punishment inflicted on the Christians in the official persecutions that we see what persecution really meant. H. B. Workman in *Persecution in the Early Church* has a summary of the terrors which the Christians had to face. "If," he writes, "we confine ourselves to strictly historical cases, the savagery, though to a large extent part of the judicial process of the age, is appalling. Some, suffering the punishment of parricides, were shut up in a sack with snakes and thrown into the sea; others were tied to huge stones and cast into a river. For Christians the cross itself was not deemed sufficient agony; hanging on trees, they were beaten with rods until their bowels gushed out, while vinegar and salt were rubbed into their wounds. In the Thebias, during the persecution of Diocletian, Christians were tied to catapults, and so wrenched limb from limb. Some, like Ignatius, were thrown to the beasts; other tied to their horns. Women were stripped, enclosed in nets, and exposed to the attacks of furious bulls. Many were ' made to lie on sharp shells ', and tortured with scrapers, claws and pincers before being delivered to the mercy of the flames. Not a few were broken on the wheel, or torn in pieces by wild horses. Of some the feet were slowly burned away, cold water being poured over them the while lest the victims should expire too rapidly. Peter, one of the servants of Diocletian, was scourged to the bone, then placed near a gridiron that he might witness the roasting of pieces of flesh torn from his own body. At Lyons they tried to overcome the obstinacy of Sanctus of Vienne ' by fixing red-hot plates to the most delicate parts of his body '. Down the backs of others ' melted lead, hissing and bubbling,' was poured; while a few, by the clemency of the Emperor, escaped with the searing out of their eyes, or the tearing off of their legs . . . . to say nothing of the rack, the hobby-horse, the claws, and other tortures preparatory to sentence."

These are not pretty or pleasant experiences to visualise, but it is well to remember that Christianity both in the human and the divine sense is a blood-bought faith.

Let us briefly return again to the reasons for this persecution. We have already seen how the political demand of Cæsar worship dominated the situation; but that demand for persecution on the part of the authorities could hardly have succeeded and could hardly have been continued, unless it had had, at least to some extent, public opinion behind it.

The main cause of the hatred of the Christians was the fact that they were different. The word which is used to describe the Christian in the New Testament itself is intensely significant. It is the word *hagios;* that is the word which is so often translated *saints*. It is also the word whose standard meaning is *holy*. The root meaning of this word is *different*. That which is *hagios,* holy, is different from other things. The Temple is holy because it is different from other buildings; the Sabbath day is holy because it is different from other days. The Christian is, therefore, a person who is fundamentally *different*. Now, if that difference had been expressed by withdrawal from life, there might well have been dislike, but it is improbable that the dislike would have issued in persecution. But the Christian difference was a difference which was expressed within the world. Paul does not write to the saints in the desert, or to the saints in a monastery; he writes to the saints in Philippi and in Rome. It was, therefore, inevitable that the Christians daily confronted the heathen with this difference in their lives.

Further, the difference which was expressed in the life of the Christian was a difference which was a constant unspoken criticism and condemnation of the pagan way of life. It was not that the Christian went about criticising and condemning and disapproving; nor was it that the Christian was consciously self-righteous and superior. It was simply that the Christian ethic in itself was a criticism and condemnation of pagan life and standards. People will always seek to eliminate that which silently condemns them. One of the most famous of all early Athenian statesmen was Aristides, who was called the Just. In the end he was banished, not for any crime, but simply because the people were humiliated and abased at the sight of the goodness of the man. Plutarch tells of the time when the people were voting on whether or not he was to be banished. Those who voted for his banishment had to write his name on an *ostracon,* a piece of pottery. An illiterate fellow, who did not know Aristides even by sight, approached Aristides himself, and, being unable to write, asked him to write *Aristides* on the *ostracon* and so to enable him to record his vote for banishment. Aristides asked him if Aristides had ever done him an injury which made him vote for his banishment. "None at all," said the man. "I do not even know this man; but I am tired of hearing him everywhere called the Just." The existence of a just man was in itself an offence. There was a surprising friendship between Alcibiades, the brilliant but debauched young Athenian, and Socrates. But sometimes Alcibiades would say to Socrates: "Socrates, I hate you; for when I am with you I realize what I am."

The Christians were persecuted because the difference in their lives was a daily rebuke to many of the pagans. Peter says that the heathen spoke evil of the Christians for no other reason than that the Christians did not run with them to the same excess of riot (I Peter 4. 4). It is an abiding fact in the human situation that the Christian will always be liable to persecution of one kind or another for the reason that the Christian is bound to be the conscience of whatever community of which he may be a member. The Christian does not even need to speak; his presence and his life are a conscience to the sphere, the society, the circle in which he moves. It is not a matter of spoken criticism and constant fault-finding; it is not a matter of conscious superiority; it is simply that the existence of the Christian life is a reminder of what life ought to be and a condemnation of the world as it is. It is no new thing for a man to seek to silence his conscience. The Christian as the conscience of the community must be exposed to the dislike, the hatred, and the attack of that part of the world which lives without God.

What, then, is the Christian defence against this persecution and this attack? It is a notable and an extremely important and significant fact that in the great early days of the Church the Christian never conceived of the possibility of using force to meet persecution. It was not long before the Christians were so numerous that concerted Christian action might well have overturned the Roman government. But the Christian did not believe that Christianity could be defended by the use of any kind of force. Against persecution the Christian had two weapons. First, he had the weapon of the Christian life. It is the appeal of Peter that the Christians should silence the slanders of the world by living so finely that these slanders should be demonstrated to be untrue. The Christian must show himself so loyal and so useful a citizen, and so good and so conscientious a servant, that the slanders of the heathen should be silenced (I Peter 2. 12-18). The Christian must have so good a conscience that he will put to shame those who make any accusation against him (I Peter 3. 13-16). In the days of persecution the Church grasped one great principle which remains for ever valid and true—the only effective Christian propaganda is the propaganda of a good life; the only defence of Christianity is the Christian. Second, the Christian had the defence of Christian apologetic. It was Peter's insistence that the Christian must ever be ready to give an answer to any man who asks him a reason for the hope that is in him (I Peter 3. 15). That is to say, if the Christian is to meet an attack on the Christian faith, he must know what he believes and why he believes it.

The only weapons which the Christian can use against any kind of persecution are the demonstration of the Christian life, and the intelligent presentation of the Christian belief.

In regard to persecution we have one question still left to ask. How can we speak of the blessedness of the persecuted? How can we speak of the bliss of the martyr's pain? On the face of it it seems strange and contradictory and paradoxical, and yet, when we come to think about it, it is not difficult to see that there is a joy in persecution, a joy which is specifically the martyr's joy.

Persecution is in fact a compliment. To persecute a person is to show that we take him so seriously that we consider that he must be eliminated. No one will persecute a person who is futile, ineffective, and indecisive. Persecution only comes to the man whose life is so positive and real in its effectiveness that society regards him as a danger. George Bernard Shaw said that the finest compliment the world can pay an author is to burn his books, because the world thereby shows that it regards these books as so dynamic and explosive that they cannot be allowed to continue to affect the minds of men. Persecution is always a proof of the utter genuineness and sincerity of the faith of the man who is persecuted. A time-serving, compromising, facing-both-ways, hypocritical, uncommitted Christian will never be persecuted. To be persecuted is to be complimented as a real Christian.

Persecution is an opportunity to demonstrate loyalty. It is when things become difficult that there comes the acid test of the loyalty of the Christian. Persecution gives to the Christian the opportunity to show that he is not ashamed of the gospel of Christ, and that he does not shrink from showing whose he is and whom he serves.

To be persecuted is to walk in the way of the saints, the prophets and the martyrs. " So persecuted they the prophets which were before you " (Matthew 5. 12). To be amongst the persecuted is to have the thrill of knowing that we are one of the great company of those whose names are on the honour-roll of the faith.

To endure persecution is undoubtedly the way to satisfaction. Time and time again the verdict of history is with the persecuted and not the persecutor. James Russell Lowell, the American poet, wrote in his poem called *The Present Crisis*:

> Truth for ever on the scaffold, Wrong for ever
>   on the throne,
> Yet that scaffold sways the future, and, behind
>   the dim unknown,
> Standeth God within the shadow, keeping
>   watch above His own.

But—and it can be even more important—the brave and loyal acceptance of persecution enables a man to meet his own verdict upon his own self. The Stoics used to argue that in the last analysis a man instinctively knows and admits that he would rather do the right and accept persecution than do the wrong and escape persecution. They use a famous illustration. In Greek history there were two famous men called Harmodius and Aristogeiton who plotted and planned against tyranny and for freedom. Their plan was discovered; they were arrested and killed. Both of them had been friendly with a famous Athenian courtesan, an *hetaira,* called Laeaena,

which means Lioness. After the arrest and death of
Harmodius and Aristogeiton Laeaena too was arrested,
and every effort was made to compel her to divulge the
names of others who were implicated in the plot.
Laeaena was so determined to keep faith with her former
friends and clients that under torture she deliberately bit
out her tongue, lest she should speak. So in memory of
her the Athenians erected a famous bronze statue of a
tongueless lioness. The Stoics posed the question,
Whether would you rather be Laeaena in the days of
her luxury and her pleasure and her cushioned ease,
or in the hour when she bit out her tongue rather
than be disloyal to those who had called her friend?
There is no doubt as to the answer to that question.
Instinctively the heart of man sides with Laeaena in her
torture.

The history of the Church of England has an outstanding example of this principle in action. Thomas
Cranmer was archbishop of Canterbury; he had leanings
towards Protestantism and he was closely affiliated to the
Protestants. When Mary came to the throne, and began
her persecuting career in her attempt to obliterate
Protestantism, Cranmer was arrested. Thereupon to
save his life he signed no fewer than six recantations of
all his connection with Protestantism. His recantations
did not in the end succeed in saving his life; but when
the time came to die, Cranmer found a new courage. In
St. Mary's Church in Oxford he was brought forward to
repeat his recantations. Instead of doing so he ended his
address to the deeply moved congregation: "Now I
come to the great thing that troubleth my conscience

more than any other thing I said or did in my life, and
that is the setting abroad of writings contrary to the truth,
which here I now renounce and refuse as things written
by my hand contrary to the truth I thought in my heart,
and written for fear of death to save my life, if it might
be. And forasmuch as my hand offended in writing
contrary to my heart, my hand, therefore, shall be the
first punished; for, if I come to the fire, it shall be the
first burned." And, when he did come to the stake,
he held out his hand and put it into the flames saying:
"This was the hand that wrote it, therefore, it shall
suffer first punishment." And, holding it steadily in the
flames, " he never stirred nor cried till life was gone."
For Cranmer the joy of martyrdom was far greater than
the joy of escape. To evade persecution may be to escape
trouble for the moment, but in the end it is to beget that
self-contempt which makes life intolerable. To face
persecution may bring the agony of the moment, but in
the end it is the way to satisfaction and to peace of heart.

All through the New Testament there runs the
conviction that to accept and to endure persecution places
a man in a special relationship with Jesus Christ. To
accept undeserved suffering and persecution is to follow
the example of Christ and to walk in His steps (I Peter
2. 21-24). The suffering which faith and loyalty bring
is for his sake (Philippians 1. 29). In this connection the
thought of the New Testament can be very bold. To
suffer for the faith is to be a partaker, a sharer, in the
sufferings of Jesus Christ (I Peter 4. 13-16). It is in
Paul that we find the greatest thought of all. To suffer
for the faith is to " fill up that which is behind of the

afflictions of Christ" (Colossians 1. 24). It is as if that when the Christian suffers, he suffers that which is lacking in the sufferings of Christ, as if he completed the full total of the sufferings of Christ. What can that mean? How can there be anything incomplete or lacking in the sufferings of Christ?

When some great discovery which affects the health and the welfare of man has been made by a scientist in his laboratory, or by a doctor in his surgery, it has still to be made available to men and women in general. The discovery is itself only half the battle; the making of it available is just as important; and it often happens that the making of it available involves a long battle with ignorance and prejudice and hostility and opposition. It has often happened that the cost of making some discovery available was greater than the cost of the initial discovery. Here we have an analogy to the position of the work of Christ and of our share in it. The Christ-deed is completed and done; the Cross is endured and the victory is won. But the news of what Christ did, and the offer of salvation in Christ has still to be brought to all men. The bringing of that news can be costly. It can involve sacrifice and suffering and martyrdom and death; and all that suffering can in a real sense be said to be the completing of the suffering of Christ, for without it the sacrifice of Christ can never be known to men. Further, Jesus Christ lived and died to make this world a certain kind of world for men and women; he lived and died that men and women everywhere should not only know salvation and the forgiveness of sins and peace with God, but also that they should live a life

of health and happiness and liberty and freedom such
as befits sons and daughters of God to live. It has cost
many and many a sacrifice, and it will continue so to do,
to make the kind of society and the kind of world to
which the name Christian can be given; but such a
world and such a society were the aim of Christ, and he
who toils and labours and suffers and endures to make
such a world is in a real sense sharing in filling up and
completing the sufferings of Jesus Christ. The greatest
thought of all is that he who suffers for the faith and for
the betterment of the men and women for whom Christ
died is a sharer in the sufferings of Christ and is even
filling up that which is still lacking in the sufferings of
his Lord.

The ultimate reward of such suffering is clear. Jesus
Christ will be in no man's debt. He who is partaker in
the sufferings of Christ will inevitably share in the glory
of Christ. If we suffer with him, we shall be glorified
with him (Romans 8. 17). To be partakers of the
suffering is to be partakers of the consolation (II
Corinthians 1. 7). If we suffer with him, we shall also
reign with him (II Timothy 2. 12). The essence of
Christianity is union with Christ, and that union will
necessarily involve union with his sufferings and union
with his glory.

THE EPILOGUE

We have studied and thought our way through the Beatitudes and now there remain two things to say. One of them is a warning, and the other is an encouragement.

i. Let us begin with the warning. It is to be noted to whom the Beatitudes and the whole Sermon on the Mount are addressed. They are addressed to the *disciples* (Matthew 5. 1). That is to say, the Beatitudes and the Sermon on the Mount describe a way of life which is only addressed to, and only possible for, the committed Christian.

We frequently hear people saying that the world would enter into a new and perfect age of peace and love, if only people would live according to the teaching of the Beatitudes and of the Sermon on the Mount. Lionel Curtis insists that the Church must never be regarded as an end in itself, but as the means and instrument towards what he calls the realization of the Commonwealth of God upon earth. He goes on to say that, if he is asked to define what he means by that Commonwealth, his answer is: "The Sermon on the Mount reduced to political terms." The way to the perfect world is the acceptance and the living of the teaching of the Sermon on the Mount.

The next step taken by so many is to say: "Let us have the Christian ethic without minding about the

Christian theology. Let us have the ethic without bothering about the religion. Let us have the ethic without thinking about who Jesus was, or about the claims which he made upon men."

The answer to this is that the Christian ethic is only possible for the committed Christian. The proof of that statement is obvious. The world has had the Sermon on the Mount and the Christian ethic clear before it for almost two thousand years and it is no nearer to achieving it and working it out in practice. It still remains a dream and a vision. The plain truth is that the Christian ethic is completely impossible without the Christian dynamic.

There is in this world an obvious difference between *ought* and *can*. There is all the difference in the world between what a man ought to do in theory and what he can do in fact. It may be perfectly correct to say to a fat, flabby, out of condition, middle-aged man that he *ought* to be able to run the hundred yards race in ten seconds, but the plain fact is that he cannot do so. When we think of a world in terms of men and women living and acting towards each other on the basis of the Sermon on the Mount, the whole dream is a complete impossibility without that committal to Jesus Christ from which the ability to live this kind of life springs. Only he who gave us his commands can enable us to obey these commands. The Christian ethic is a complete impossibility without Christ. There is no such thing in this world as Christian power and Christian living without Christian commitment. It is not the Christian ethic which makes Christian men and women; it is Christian men and women who can live the Christian ethic. The Sermon on the Mount, the essence of the Christian ethic, was addressed to those who were disciples; and the Christian ethic can never be divorced from commitment to Jesus Christ.

ii. But there is also encouragement here. The disciples were disciples before Jesus taught them. They had not waited to understand everything before they linked their lives to the life of Jesus Christ. They linked their lives to him and then he taught them.

There are many people who refuse to commit themselves to Jesus Christ and to his Church because they do not understand this or that doctrine, or because there are certain things in Christianity which are a mystery to them. There is no one in this world who understands the whole of Christianity. G. K. Chesterton said long ago that only the fool tries to get the heavens into his head, in which case his head not unnaturally bursts; the Christian man and the wise man is quite content to get his head inside the heavens.

Once Jesus said a very relevant thing. "If any man will do his will, he shall know of the doctrine" (John 7. 17). If we start out on the Christian way, even if we are well aware that our understanding of the Christian doctrine is very imperfect and very inadequate, it will become clearer to us the more we do the will of God as we know it. The old Latin tag has it: *Solvitur ambulando*. The problems clear up as we go ahead. The man who waits to understand everything will wait for ever. We must begin with what we know and as we go on we will understand more and more.

The ideal is there. The way to the ideal is committal to Jesus Christ; and for that committal we do not need to wait for perfect understanding; we can begin with love.

THE LORD'S PRAYER

IN MEMORY OF MY CHIEF
G.H.C.M.
A MAN OF PRAYER

FOREWORD

The greater part of this book appeared as series of articles in the Preacher's Quarterly, and I have to thank the editor and publisher of that magazine for permission to reprint the articles in the form of this little book.

It might seem that there is nothing new that anyone can say about the Lord's Prayer, and doubtless that is true. But just because of the frequency with which it is used the Lord's Prayer is always in danger of becoming a vain repetition, and, if this book does no more than remind people what they are doing when they pray the greatest of all prayers, and if it makes them think a little more when they take the words of that prayer upon their lips, then it will have more than served its purpose.

WILLIAM BARCLAY

University of Glasgow

INTRODUCTION

WHAT WILL I SAY?

Often, when we had a letter to write when we were very young, we would go to our parents or to some older person and ask: "What will I say?" And many of us, perhaps indeed most of us, remain like that all our lives. In the East the letter-writer was a professional figure. There he sat with his little desk and his pot of ink and his pen, and, if anyone wanted a letter written, it was to the letter-writer that he went. People needed some one to tell them what to say. In our countries we can go into a shop and buy a manual of letter-writing, a handbook which will give us specimen letters to show us what to say on different occasions.

When we ask: "What will I say?" we do not really mean quite that. We know quite well *what* we want to say. We may want to send a word of thanks for a gift or for a kindness; we may want to send a request for help or for information; we may want to send a message of friendship or good-will or love; we may want to send our good wishes or our sympathy or our congratulations or even our complaints. This much we know. The problem that most people have is not to know *what* to say but to know *how* to say it. Very few people are really articulate; most people have real difficulty in putting their thoughts into words, and still more difficulty in putting their feelings into words.

If a person who wants to know: "What will I say?"

goes to some one and asks that question, it is not much help to be given the answer: " Oh, just sit down and write." This is exactly what the person cannot do. This is precisely his problem. He wants to know how he can get down on paper and into words the things he knows he ought to say. It is the same with making a speech. Often some one who has to make a speech at a wedding reception or at some other such function will go to some one who is good at making speeches and say: " I've got to make a speech at a wedding. Tell me what to say." He knows quite well that he wants to convey his own and other people's good wishes and kind thoughts and congratulations, but his problem is how to do it and how to set about it, and it is not much help to him to say: " Just get up and talk." If he could do that, he would not be asking for help.

When a person comes with this request, " What will I say?" there are two ways in which he can be given help. The person helping can simply dictate the letter or the speech for him to write down, or can write it out for him to copy. That is one way to help, but it is not the best way to help, for if help is given in that way, the letter will be some one else's letter, and the speech will be some one else's speech. It will no doubt say all the right and the necessary things, but it may well say them in a way and in a style that the person who needed the help would never have used himself. The personal and the individual touch will be quite lacking.

But there is another way to help. The person needing help may be given, not a dictated letter or speech to repeat and to copy without alteration, but rather an outline and a pattern, which will be a guide through which he is enabled to express things in his own way. This is far the better way, for in this way the person is enabled to say the right things, but to say them in his own way.

It is exactly this that happened with Jesus and his disciples in regard to prayer. They wanted to pray; they knew their own needs and desires; they knew that God could satisfy them; but they really did not know how to set about praying. " Lord," they said, " teach us to pray " (Luke 11.1). " When you·pray," said Jesus, " pray like this," and he taught them the Lord's Prayer (Luke 11.2; Matthew 6.9). But what he was doing was that he was giving them a pattern of prayer far more than a form of words which they were to do no more than repeat, like children reciting a lesson.

The experience of the disciples is the experience of very many of us. We wish to pray for we know well that we need God. But we hardly know how to start; and we do not know how to put it. And Jesus, just as he gave it to his disciples, gives us in the Lord's Prayer, not only a prayer to repeat in itself, but a prayer to be for us the pattern of our own prayers.

And the pattern is very simple but very comprehensive. In the Lord's Prayer Jesus says to us :

When you pray,

> Remember that God is your Father and your King, and that, therefore, you go to One in whom Love and Power are equally combined.

When you pray,

> Do not hesitate to tell God about your daily needs.

When you pray,

> Do not shrink from telling God about your mistakes.

When you pray,

> Never forget to place the unknown future and all its perils in the hands of God.

In the Lord's Prayer in answer to his disciples' request
Jesus gave to them and gave to us a prayer which is
at one and the same time a prayer to use by itself and
a pattern for all prayer.

A PRAYING PEOPLE

There could be nothing more natural than that one of Jesus's disciples should come to him and ask him to teach them how to pray (Luke 11.1), for the Jews were characteristically and pre-eminently a praying people.

They came to God with an absolute confidence that God desired their prayers and that God would hear. "The Holy One," said the Rabbis, "yearns for the prayers of the righteous." "The Lord is near to all who call upon him," said the Psalmist, "to all who call upon him in truth" (Psalm 145.18). "They cried to the Lord in their trouble, and he delivered them from their distress" (Psalm 107.6). "When he calls to me," says God of the good man, "I will answer him" (Psalm 91.15). For that reason we will do well to see the Jewish heritage of prayer into which the disciples had entered before they ever received the teaching and the example of Jesus.

No Jew ever doubted the power of prayer. "Prayer, the weapon of the mouth," said the Rabbis, "is mighty."[1] No Jew ever doubted that God's ear and heart were open to the prayer of all his children. "All are equal when they pray before God, women and slaves, sage and simpleton, poor and rich."[2] Though all the world should pray at once, God will hear the prayer of each one. They quoted the verse, "O thou

[1] Tanh. Beshallah 9. f. iiia.
[2] Quoted I. Abrahams: *Studies in Pharisaism and the Gospels*, Second Series, 82.

that hearest prayer, unto thee shall all flesh come"
(Psalm 65.2). Then they went on to say: "A human
king can hearken to two or three people at once,
but he cannot hearken to more; God is not so, for all
men may pray to him, and he hearkens to them all
simultaneously. Men's ears become satisfied with hearing; but God's ears are never satiated. He is never
wearied by men's prayers."[3] Nor is God ever bored by
the continual coming of his children. There is a
rabbinic parable: "A man visits his friend and his
friend greets him cordially, placing him on the couch
beside him. He comes again, and is given a chair.
He comes again and receives a stool. He comes a fourth
time and the friend says, 'The stool is too far off,
I cannot fetch it for you.' But God is not so. For
whenever Israel knocks at the door of God's house,
the Holy One rejoices, as it is written; For what great
nation is there that hath a God so nigh unto them
as our God is, *whenever* we call?"[4] To a man a friend
may be less and less welcome on each visit, until
he becomes a nuisance, but it is never so with God.

Once the Temple had been destroyed in A.D. 70, and
once sacrifice became for ever impossible for the Jew,
prayer became the supreme sacrifice and offering; but
even before that there were many Rabbis who would
have held that prayer is greater in the sight of God
than sacrifice. "God said to Israel, Be assiduous in
regard to devotion, for there is no finer quality than
prayer. Prayer is greater than all the sacrifices."[5] "In
the law of the sacrifices it says, If a man has a bullock
let him offer a bullock; if not, let him give a ram,
or a lamb, or a pigeon; and if he cannot afford a
pigeon, let him bring a handful of flour. And if he

3 *Midrash* on Psalm 65.
4 *Midrash* on Psalm 4: *T. B. Yoma* 76a.
5 Isaiah I. 11, 13: Tanh. Wayera I, f 31b.

has not even any flour, let him bring nothing at all, but come with words of prayer."[6]

As the Jewish teachers saw it, prayer should be constant, and not simply when a man is in need. The Talmud uses as an illustration the saying in Ecclesiasticus, "Honour the physician *before* you have need of him," and goes on to comment: "The Holy One says, Just as it is my office to cause the rain and the dew to fall, and make the plants to grow to sustain man, so art thou bounden to pray before me, and to praise me in accordance with my works; thou shalt not say, I am in prosperity, wherefore shall I pray? But when misfortune befalls me then will I come and supplicate. Before misfortune comes, anticipate and pray."[7] Prayer is not so much an emergency appeal in need as it is a continuing and unbroken conversation and fellowship with God.

Friedländer very beautifully sets out the feelings in the heart which lead a man to pray.[8] We ought to take everything that is in our hearts and lay it before God. By that very fact we are compelled to examine the desires of our hearts, to see whether they contain anything that is unholy, unjust or ignoble. "Prayer has the salutary effect of purifying, refining, and ennobling our heart. It banishes evil thoughts, and thus saves us much pain and sorrow."[9] Let us then see, as Friedländer put it for his people, the feelings of the heart which we should bring to God.

We should bring our *love*. "I will bless the Lord at all times: his praise shall continually be in my mouth" (Psalm 34.2). "O Lord, open my lips; and my mouth shall show forth thy praise" (Psalm 51.17).

[6] Hosea 14.2: Tanh. B. Zaw, viii, 9a.
[7] Ecclesiasticus 33.31: Exod. R. ch. xxiii.
[8] M. Friedländer, *The Jewish Religion* 280-284.
[9] M. Friedländer, *The Jewish Religion* 183.

Clearly, we should bring our *gratitude* and our *thanksgiving*. " I will praise thee, for thou hast heard me " (Psalm 118.21). " I will sacrifice unto thee with the voice of thanksgiving " (Jonah 2.9). As one of the Rabbis had it : " Though all prayers were to be discontinued, prayers of thanksgiving will never be discontinued." And yet we must have a care that we thank God for the right things. "When thy enemy falls, do not rejoice." The Talmud has a very lovely passage : " The Angels wished to sing praises to God while the Egyptians were drowning in the sea, and God rebuked them saying, Shall I listen to your hymns when my children are perishing before my eyes?"[10] As the Jewish teachers saw it, no man can ever give God thanks for the misfortune of any other man. Always when a man prays he must have in his mind the *holiness* of God. However much a man comes to God in love and in trust and in confidence, there must still be that reverence which will prevent an undue familiarity on the part of the creature before his Creator. " In his prayer," said Rabbi Simon, " a man should think that the Shechinah (i.e. the glory of God) is before him.[11]"

When a man has in his mind the holiness of God, as he prays, there must of necessity be two other things in his mind. There must be *the desire to obey and to please God*. " How sweet are thy words to my taste," said the Psalmist, " sweeter than honey to my mouth !" " My tongue will sing of thy word, for all thy commandments are right " (Psalm 119. 103, 172). There will be *the fear to offend God*. It is only the man with clean hands and a pure heart who can ascend into the hill of the Lord (Psalm 24.3,4). It is the Psalmist's determination : " I will wash mine hands in innocence, and go about thine altar, O Lord " (Psalm

[10] T. B. Yebamoth 64a.   [11] San. 22a.

26.6). Above all, in prayer a man will take all his weakness to the strength of God. A man is only too well aware of the insecurity of life, of his helplessness in face of the chances and the changes of life, of the way in which the light can suddenly turn to darkness. "The Lord," said the Psalmist, "is a stronghold for the oppressed, a stronghold in time of trouble" (Psalm 9.9). As the Talmud had it : "Even when the edge of the sword already touches a man's neck, even then he must not abandon his faith in praying to God."[12] "Hope in the Lord and pray again."[13]

There are still other things which we must note about the Jewish idea of prayer that we may see still more clearly the heritage which the disciples already possessed before Jesus taught them to pray.

A great part of prayer was *penitence*. "The gate of tears is never shut."[14] Even if the congregation can bring nothing else, they can weep and pray and God will receive them.[15] To the prayer of penitence the Jews attribute a quite extraordinary power. The Jew was always fascinated by what we may call the paradox of God. The decrees of God are immutable; his laws are inviolable; his judgments are inevitable. It would, therefore, seem that God's condemnation of the sinner is quite unalterable. And yet the fact remains true that there is such a thing as the wonder of the mercy of God. The Jew literally believed that the prayer of the penitent heart could turn the wrath of God into the mercy of God. "Why is the prayer of the righteous like a rake? As the rake turns the grain from place to place, so the prayer of the righteous turns the attribute of mercy."[16] Rabbi Ishmael once when he was acting as a priest entered into the innermost sanctuary to burn incense. There he saw God, and prayed to

[12] T. B. Ber. 5a. [13] R. Deut. ii. [14] T. B. Ber. 32b.
[15] R. Exod. xxviii. 4. [16] Yeb. 64a.

God, "May it be thy will that thy mercy subdue thy wrath," and God nodded in assent.[17] Perhaps the most astonishing picture in all Jewish religious writing is the picture of God praying to himself that his mercy may prevail. Rab said that the prayer of God ran thus : " May it be my will that my compassion may overcome mine anger, and that it may prevail over my attributes of justice and judgment, and that I may deal with my children according to the attribute of compassion, and that I may not act towards them according to the strict line of justice."[18] Israel Abrahams quotes the line of Solomon Ibn Gabirol in his *Royal Crown,* " the most inspired hymn after the Psalter " : "From thee I fly to thee."[19] Surely this is the most vivid of all ways of saying that it did not cost God nothing to forgive sin.

The highest prayer is always *the prayer of the community.* The prayer of an individual always tends to be, or runs the risk of being, selfish; and, therefore, the highest kind of prayer is the prayer of the community, from which a man must never separate himself. " Israel will be redeemed only when it forms one single band : when all are united they will receive the presence of the Shechinah."[20] It is only that man who shares in the troubles of the community, as Moses shared in the distresses of his brethren, who will see the consolation of the community.[21] When the righteous are even on the point of death they do not think of their own concerns but of the needs of the community. When Moses was told that he must die (Numbers 27.12-14), his immediate concern was not for himself, but that God should appoint another leader

---

[17] T. B. Ber. 7a.   [18] Ber. 7a.
[19] I. Abrahams, *Studies in Pharisaism and the Gospels,* Second Series, 90.
[20] Aboth 2.5.   [21] Ta'an. IIa.

in his place.[22] Perhaps the most extraordinary instance
of this line of thought is in the curious Rabbinic
prayer: "Let not the prayer of wayfarers find entrance,
O Lord, before thee."[23] The idea is that the wayfarer
might be asking for fine weather when the country
as a whole needed rain. It is not that Jewish thought
either condemned or neglected personal and private
prayer, far from it; it is simply that the Jew had
a horror of selfishness in prayer, and, therefore, stressed
the need of praying in and with the community, and
we may well remember that the words *I, me, my,* and
mine never appear in the Lord's Prayer.

The Jew strongly believed in *perseverance* in prayer.
Moses still prayed for the mercy of God, even when
God said to him, "Enough for thee, speak no more to
me of this matter!" (Deut. 3.26). How much less
should other men desist when their prayer is not
answered! After the sin of the golden calf Moses
interceded for Israel for forty days (Deut. 9.18, 25).
The Rabbis tell how Hezekiah in his mortal illness
did not give up praying even when Isaiah announced
to him in the name of the Lord that he must die and not
live (Isaiah 38.1-5). We have a family tradition, he
said to the prophet, that even if a sharp sword is resting
on a man's throat, he should not refrain from craving
mercy.[24] Prayer, repentance and almsgiving are the
three things which can cause even a decree of God
to be rescinded.[25] The Jew saw nothing wrong and
nothing unnatural in pleading with God.

Although prayer must be offered in perseverance and
in persistence, it must nonetheless be offered in *humility.*
Always the person who prayed made it clear that he
wanted nothing other than the will of God. "May

---

[22] Sifre Num. Pinehas 138f. 52a.   [23] T. Jer. Joma 5.2.
[24] Sifre Deut. 29; Ber. 10a.
[25] Jer. Ta'an. 65b; Jer. Sanh. 28c.

it be thy good pleasure to grant . . ."; "what is good in thine eyes, do," are the standard beginnings for prayer. "Learn to say, Whatever the Almighty does is done for our good."[26] No man must pray and expect an answer as a right. A haughty prayer is an abomination. There is a curious saying: "To three sins man is daily liable, thoughts of evil, *reliance on prayer*, and slander. He who prays thinking he deserves an answer, receives none."[27] The idea is that there can be a confidence in prayer which is an arrogant supposition that God *must* do what those who pray ask. An answer to prayer is always a boon and never a right. "Do not make thy prayer a fixed claim or demand, which must be fulfilled, but a supplication for mercy which may or may not be granted."[28] Even in prayer a man must remember that God is the Creator and that he is the created.

To the Jew *intercession* was specially precious. It is a prayer which is uttered on behalf of another which is always answered first.[29] Rab said: "Whoever has it in his power to pray on behalf of his neighbour, and fails to do so, is called a sinner."[30] Here is another instance of the Jewish horror of being selfish in prayer. It is at least as important to pray for others as it is to pray for oneself.

Just because prayer held so high a place in Jewish thought and life, it was specially liable to certain dangers and to certain misuses, dangers and misuses which were much in Jesus' mind when he spoke to his disciples about prayers. The one supreme danger was the danger of *formalism*. Just because the Jews were so anxious to see that prayer was never omitted, that it was

[26] Ber. 6ob.
[27] Ber. 32b; 55a; Baba Bathra 164b; Rosh Hashanah 18a.
[28] Aboth. 2.13.   [29] Baba Quama 92a.   [30] Ber. 12b.

given its proper place in life, the tendency was to sur-
round it with rules and regulations. And yet very many
writers are quite unfair to the Jews in dealing with this
matter for two reasons. First, such formalism as there was
sprang entirely from the determination and the desire
to give prayer its proper place in life. Second, there
was no one more aware of the dangers than the Jews
themselves, and in their finest thought they lay down the
very laws by which the formalism can be overcome,
and by which in so many cases it was overcome.
Schürer writes: "Even prayer itself, that centre of
religious life, was bound in the fetters of a rigid
mechanism."[81] There is truth there, but it is only
half the truth, and we will go on to look at the dangers,
but we will not forget the ideals behind them, for,
as Aristotle said long ago, any person or any institution
must be judged by his and its best and highest manifestation.

i. There was formalism in regard to *time*. The devout
Jew prayed three times a day, at 9 a.m., at 12 noon, and
at 3 p.m. With the characteristic Jewish desire to
trace things as far back as possible, the morning prayer
was ascribed to Abraham (Genesis 19.27); the afternoon prayer to Isaac (Genesis 24.63); and the evening
service to Jacob (Genesis 28.11). Daniel, too, prayed
three times a day looking toward Jerusalem (Daniel
6.10). It is quite true that this could become a sheer
formalism, and that it could become an opportunity for
ostentation, for, wherever a man was at the hours of
prayer, he prayed, and he might well deliberately
choose a place where as many as possible might
see him. David, too, said, "At evening, at morning,
and at noon, will I pray and cry aloud" (Psalm 55.17).
This could, of course, become a ritual prayer cycle;

[81] E. Schürer: *History of the Jewish People in the Time of
Christ*, 2.2. 115.

but it is also true that the devout Jew could say:
"Would that man were capable of praying continuously, all day long!"[82]

ii. There was formalism in regard to *place*. Just as a
man had to pray at the right time, so also he had
to pray in the right place. Abba Benjamin said:
"A man's prayer is only heard by God when offered
in a Synagogue."[83] Rabbi Huna said: "Who ever
fixes a place for prayer, has the God of Abraham
for his help."[84] Rabbi Jochanan said that a man should
have a place exclusively kept for prayer.[85] Peter and
John were going up to the Temple at three o'clock
in the afternoon "at the hour of prayer" when they
came upon the lame man at the Beautiful Gate and
healed him (Acts 3.1). But it would be very wrong to
take that as the only rule of Jewish prayer. This very
same Rabbi Jochanan said that the man who prays
in his house surrounds it with a wall of iron[86]—which
is one of the loveliest things ever said about family
worship. And there is a Midrash on one of the Psalms
which says: "God says to Israel: Pray in the Synagogue
of your city; if you cannot, pray in the field; if you
cannot, pray in your house; if you cannot, pray on your
bed; if you cannot, commune with your own heart
upon your bed and be still."[87] There is nowhere where
God cannot be found. Even if a working man was
working on the top of a tree, or on a scaffolding against
a building, it was permitted to pray at the hour of
prayer just where he was.[88] In any Synagogue it
was the rule to pray facing towards Jerusalem, and in
the Temple it was the rule to pray facing the Holy
of Holies; and yet at the same time it must be

[82] Tan. B., Mikkez 98a—98b.   [83] Ber. 6a.   [84] Ber. 6b.
[85] Jer. Ber. 8b.   [86] Jer. Ber. 8d.
[87] Midrash Psalms iv. 9. 23b; Pesickta 158b.
[88] M. Ber. 4.4.

remembered that the Rabbis could say: "A blind man, or one who is unable to locate the directions, should direct his heart to his Father in Heaven."[39] True, there could be formalism in regard to place, but beyond the formalism there was the certainty that God does not dwell in any Temple made with hands.

iii. There was formalism in regard to the *set forms* of prayer. The greatest of all Jewish prayers is the *Shemoneh 'Esreh,* which means The Eighteen. It consisted of eighteen prayers in the form of benedictions, all with the phrase, "Blessed be thou." It was called the *Tefillah,* which means The Prayer, as it were, *par excellence.* It was part of every Jewish Synagogue service, and every devout Jew was to pray it three times a day. There was even an "abstract" of it, which might be used when a man could not pray the full prayer: "Give us understanding, O Lord our God, to know thy ways; to circumcise our hearts, to fear thee, and forgive us so that we may be redeemed. Keep us far from sorrow. Satiate us on the pastures of thy land, and gather our scattered ones from the four corners of the earth. Let the righteous rejoice in the rebuilding of thy city and in the establishment of thy Temple, and in the flourishing of the horn of David, thy servant, and in the clear-shining light of the son of Jesse, thine anointed. Even before we call, do thou answer. Blessed art thou, O Lord, who hearkenest unto prayer."[40]

There were set prayers for all the events of life. These prayers are set out in the treatise in the Mishnah called *Berachoth,* which means Benedictions. At the sight of fruits, or wine, or vegetables, or any of the produce of the earth, a man should say: "Blessed art thou who createst the fruit of the tree, the fruit of the vine, the fruit of the earth." (6.1). If a man sees

[39] Ber. 30a. [40] Ber. 29a.

shooting stars, earthquakes, lightnings, thunders and storms, he should say: "Blessed is he whose power and might fill the world." When he sees mountains, hills, rivers, deserts, he should say: "Blessed is the author of creation." For rain and good tidings, he should say: "Blessed is he, the good and the doer of good." At bad tidings, he should say: "Blessed is he, the true judge." If he has built a house or acquired anything new he should say: "Blessed is he who hath given us life." A man should pray every time he enters and leaves a city (9.1-4). It is easy to see how such a custom and a ritual might well become a formality, and little more than a kind of use of magic incantations, but surely it is equally easy to see how a man who had such habits of prayer necessarily lived in a world which was full of God, a world in which there was nothing and no event which did not turn his heart to Almighty God, the Creator and the Sustainer of all life.

iv. There was formality in regard to *length*, and Jesus did warn against "much speaking" (Matthew 6.7). But the Jewish rabbinic teaching was very much on the side of Jesus. Rabbi Me'ir said: "A man's words should always be few towards God."[41] Rabbi Chijja ben Abba said: "Whoever prolongs his prayer, and calculates on it (that is, anticipates its fulfilment as a reward for its length), will eventually come to pain of heart."[42]

In this the Rabbis were very wise, for they held that there is a time to shorten and a time to lengthen. Thus in regard to Miriam, Moses prayed no more than, "Lord, heal her," (Numbers 12.13), and yet Moses could also say, "I worshipped before the Lord forty days and forty nights" (Deuteronomy 9.18).[48] The

[41] Ber. 61a.   [42] Ber. 32b.   [48] Mechilta 29a.

Rabbis would have approved of long and ostentatious prayers no more than Jesus did. It is perfectly true that sometimes Jewish prayers pile up titles in address to God as the second section of the *Kaddish* does: " Blessed, praised and glorified, exalted, extolled, honoured, magnified and lauded, be the name of the Holy One." But the rabbinic teaching was that it was proper to apply three adjectives to God—great, mighty and revered.[44]

There are sayings on the other side : " Whenever the righteous make their prayer long, their prayer is heard."[45] " Would that a man could pray all day long."[46] But such sayings speak of the prayer of the loving heart, and of the man who continuously seeks the presence of God.

It is easy to make the charge of formalism against Jewish prayer. We may cite passages which declare that even a slip in the correct wording of a set prayer is fatal.[47] But there could hardly be anything more unfair, for formalism is the one thing which the great Jewish teachers sought with all their hearts to avoid.

The Jews described the first necessity of prayer by an almost untranslatable word. " Prayer," they said, " needs *kawannah*."[48] *Kawannah* is concentrated intention and devotion; it is the attitude in which eyes and mind and heart are fixed on God. The demand for this attitude in prayer runs through all Jewish devotional thinking and writing. " It matters not whether you do much or little, so long as your heart is directed to heaven."[49] " Everything depends on the *kawannah* of the heart."[50] Even if a man is walking, he must stop

[44] Ber. 33b. [45] Yoma 29b. [46] Ber. 21a.
[47] Ber. 5.5 [48] Jer. Ber. 7a. [49] Ber. 17a.
[50] Meg. 20a.

to pray and "direct his heart to God in awe and fear, trembling and quaking."[51] Even the action of walking might deflect the thoughts and the intention of the heart. "He who prays must direct his heart."[52] Rab said: "He whose mind is not quieted should not pray." Rabbi Chanina was wont not to pray when he was irritated.[53] The Jew prayed standing with his hands stretched out, and Rabbi Ammi said: "Man's prayer is not accepted unless he puts his heart in his hands."[54] "Let him who prays cast his eyes downwards, but turn his heart upwards."[55] Rabbi Eleazar said: "Always let a man test himself: if he can direct his heart, let him pray; if he cannot let him not pray."[56]

Formalism was abhorrent to the devout Jew. "Prayer should not be recited as if a man were reading a document"; and to avoid that, a new prayer should be said every day.[57] As soon as prayer becomes either a fixed task or a burden, it ceases to be prayer in any real sense of the term at all.[58]

The Mishnah lays it down that a man must not stand up to pray except in a serious state of mind,[59] and then the Rabbis went on to say that a man should never come straight in from business or from a journey and pray, but that for an hour he ought to compose himself and his thoughts before he prays.

We may conclude our examination of the Jewish ideas of prayer by choosing out of very many three great Jewish prayers, which the Jews still pray, and which any Christian might take with profit upon his lips. First, there is a prayer for the night before sleeping:

[51] Tanh. Lek leak 24a.   [52] Ber. 3.6.   [53] Erub. 65a.
[54] Ta'an 8a.   [55] Yeb. 105b.   [56] Ber. 30b.
[57] J. Ber. 38a.   [58] Ber. 29b.   [59] Ber. 5.1.

Blessed art thou, O Lord our God, King of the
Universe, who makest the hands of sleep to fall
upon mine eyes, and slumber upon mine eyelids.
May it be thy will, O Lord my God, and God of
my fathers, to suffer me to lie down in peace and
to let me rise again in peace. Let not my thoughts
trouble me, nor evil dreams, nor evil fancies, but
let my rest be perfect before thee. O lighten mine
eyes lest I sleep the sleep of death, for it is thou
who givest light to the apple of the eye. Blessed
art thou, O Lord, who givest light to the whole world
in thy glory.[61]

Second, there is the prayer which Rabbi Yannai taught
his disciples to pray when they woke in the morning:

Blessed art thou, O Lord, who quickenest the
dead. May it be thy will, O Lord my God, to give
me a good heart, a good nature, a good hope,
a good eye, a good soul, a lowly soul, and a humble
spirit; may thy name not be profaned among
(or, through) us, and make us not a mockery in
the mouth of men; may our end not be cut off,
nor our hope be a vexation, and may we not need
the gifts of flesh and blood, and put not our sustenance into their hands, for their gifts are small,
and the shame they cause is great; and place our
portion in thy Law, with those who do thy will;
build up thy house, thy sanctuary, thy city, thy
temple, speedily, in our days.[62]

Lastly, there is the prayer of Rab:

May it be thy will, O Lord our God, to grant us
long life, a life of peace, a life of good, a life
of blessing, a life of sustenance, a life of bodily
vigour, a life marked by the fear of sin, a life free
from shame and reproach, a life of prosperity and

[61] Ber. 60b.   [62] T. J. Ber. 7d.

honour, and a life in which love of the Law and fear of heaven shall cling to us, a life wherein thou fulfillest the desire of the heart for good.[68]

When Jesus' disciples came to him to ask him to teach them how and what to pray they came to him out of a priceless heritage of prayer, which through him was to become even greater and even more precious.

[68] Ber. 16b.

OUR FATHER

Before we begin to study the petitions of the Lord's Prayer in detail we must stop to look at the general pattern of the prayer.

We cannot fail to see that the prayer begins by giving God his own and his proper place. The first three petitions of the prayer are for the hallowing of God's name, the coming of God's Kingdom, and the doing of God's will. It is only then that we turn to our own needs and our own requests. The great fault of prayer is that it can so easily become self-centred and self-seeking. We can be so busy thinking of what we want that we have no time to think of what God wants. We can be so concerned with our own desires that we never think of God's will. We can be so busy talking to God that we never give God the chance to talk to us. We can be so busy telling God that we never stop to listen to God.

It is precisely that kind of situation that the Lord's Prayer commands us and helps us to avoid. It begins by putting, not us, but God in the centre of the picture. The circumference can only be right when the centre is right. All other things can only take their proper place when God is given his proper place. The Lord's Prayer begins with the memory of the majesty of God, the memory of the purpose of God, and the acceptance of the will of God.

The second part of the prayer is the most comprehensive prayer that men were ever taught to pray. Let us set down its three petitions:

Give us this day our daily bread.
Forgive us our debts, as we forgive our debtors.
Lead us not into temptation, but deliver us from
    evil.

The first of these three petitions is a prayer for our
present need. The second of them is a prayer for
our *past* sin. The third of them is a prayer for our
future welfare and goodness. These three short petitions
take life, past, present and future, and lay it before
God. Food for the present, forgiveness for the past,
help for the future—all of life is brought into the
presence of God.

But these three petitions do even more than that.
When we pray the first of them, the prayer for daily
bread, we think of *God the Father,* the creator and
sustainer of all life. When we pray the second of them,
the prayer for our forgiveness, we think of *God the Son,*
the Saviour and Redeemer of all mankind and of us.
When we pray the third of them, the prayer for future
help to live without sin, we think of *God the Holy
Spirit,* the Guide, the Helper and the Protector of all
life. These three petitions bring us face to face with
Father, Son and Holy Spirit. Within their narrow
compass, and with their astonishing economy of words,
these three brief petitions take the whole of life to the
whole of God.

The pattern of the Lord's Prayer must be the pattern
of all prayer, for it begins by giving God his proper place,
and it goes on to take life's past, present and future
to God, the Father, Son, and Holy Spirit.

Now we turn to the opening words of the Lord's
Prayer, the words *Our Father.* It takes very much more
than a dictionary to define the meaning of any word.
To the definition of the dictionary there must be
added the interpretation of experience. Of no word
is that truer than of the word father. The word father

has two quite distinct meanings. It can be used in the sense of *paternity*; in that sense it simply denotes the person who is responsible for the birth of a child. In that case there is no necessary connection between the father and the child other than a physical connection. A man may be the father of a child in the paternity sense of the term, and never even set eyes on the child for whose birth his action was responsible. But the word father can be used in the sense of *fatherhood*. In that sense it describes a relationship of love and intimacy and confidence and trust between the father and the child. The Christian believes that God is father in the paternity sense of the word, in the sense that it is God who is the source of all life who gives life to any child but the unique thing about the Christian idea of God is that the Christian far more believes that God is father in the fatherhood sense of the word, for he believes that between God and men there is possible through Jesus Christ an intimate, lifelong, loving relationship in which God and man come close together. This is indeed a distinction which the Jewish teachers themselves made.

The Rabbis told a story of an orphan girl who was brought up by a good and faithful guardian. The day came when she was to be married. The Scribe who was making the necessary legal arrangements for the wedding asked her : "What is your name?" And she told him. Then the Scribe asked : "What is your father's name?" The girl was silent. "Why are you silent?" asked her guardian. The girl answered : "Because I know none other than you as a father, for he who brings up is father, not he who begets." So, the Rabbis said, the real father of Israel is not anyone who is connected with Israel by any physical connection; it is God who brought the nation up.

When we say to God, Our Father, it is not simply

paternity which is in our minds; it is the far closer
relationship of fatherhood.

When Jesus taught his disciples to pray, Our Father,
he was speaking out of a rich heritage, for the fatherhood of God was a conception that was supremely dear
to a Jew. There were sayings which were often upon
Jewish lips. " You are the sons of the Lord your
God " (Deuteronomy 14.1). "I am a father to Israel "
(Jeremiah 31.9). " Is not he (the Lord) your father, who
created you, who made you and established you?"
(Deuteronomy 32.6). " Yet, O Lord, thou art our father;
we are the clay and thou art the potter; we are all
the work of thy hand " (Isaiah 64.8). It was on texts
like these that the loving devotion of the Jews fed itself.
Their conviction of the fatherhood of God brought certain assurances to the Jews.

i. Their belief in the fatherhood of God assured them
of *the nearness of God*. Because God is father, the
Jewish saints were sure that God is always near to hear
and to answer prayer and to give his presence to his
people. There is a Jewish interpretation of the instruc-
tions to Moses for the construction of the Tabernacle
in Exodus 26.18-25. The *Shechinah* was the glory of
God which sometimes settled on the Tabernacle and
on the Temple in a luminous cloud. When God said to
Moses : " Make me a dwelling-place," Moses wondered,
for Moses well knew that the glory of God fills the
upper and the lower worlds and he could not understand how the glory of God could dwell in a dwelling-
place that he might be able to construct. But God spoke
to Moses. " Your thoughts," God said, " are not my
thoughts. Twenty boards to the north, and twenty
to the south and eight to the west are enough for me
(Exodus 26.18,20,25). And not only that, but I will
come down and confine my Shechinah in one square
yard . . . You are the children of the Lord your

God, and I am your Father (Deuteronomy 14.1; Jeremiah 31.9). It is an honour to children to be near their father, and an honour to a father to be near his children; therefore, make a house for the Father that he may dwell near his children " (Exod. R. Terumah xxxiv, 1, 3). God can confine his glory to one square yard. Just because God is Father and we are his children, even in the humblest home, even in the littlest and the barest Church, even for the most unimportant person, the glory of God is there. Anywhere the Father can be and will be with his children.

The Rabbis had another way of putting this. Rabbi Judah ben Simon said : "An idol is near yet far; God is far yet near." They asked him what he meant. "An idolater makes an idol," he said, " and sets it up in his house. So the idol is near. But one may cry unto the idol and it will not answer, therefore the idol is far. But God is far yet near." "How?" they asked him. "From here to heaven," he said, "is a journey of five hundred years; therefore God is far; but he is also near, for, if a man prays and meditates in his heart, God is near to answer his prayer " (Deuteronomy R. Wa'ethanan 11.10). Even if the dwelling place of God is in the heights of heaven, even if heaven and earth cannot contain his dazzling glory, nevertheless because God is Father he is in the smallest and the humblest dwelling and near to the simplest heart.

ii. The belief of the Jews in the fatherhood of God assured them of *the mercy of God* in judgment, and of his *willingness to accept the penitent heart*. Very beautifully it was said : "God says to Israel : For all the wonders and mighty deeds which I have wrought for you, the only reward I ask is that you should honour me as my children, and call me your Father " (Exod. R. Mishpatim, xxxii. 5). The essence of God's relationship to men is fatherhood, and the dearest wish of God is that all his children should willingly enter into that relationship.

The Jewish saints thought of God as judge, but they thought of him as a judge who was also a father. There is a Jewish passage which tells of two men who came to the judgment seat in terror of the judge and who were told to take courage. " So Israel will stand at the judgment before God, and will be afraid because of the Judge. Then the angels of the service will say to them : Fear not! Do you not recognise him? He is your fellow-citizen, as it is said, It is He who will build up my city (Isaiah 45.13). Then they will say : Fear not the Judge! Do you not recognise him? He is your kinsman, as it says, The children of Israel, the people related to Him (Psalm 148.14). Then they will say : Do you not recognise him? He is your brother, as it says, for my brethren and friends' sake (Psalm 122.8). And even more, He is your Father, as it is said, Is He not thy Father?" (Deuteronomy 32.6). Here is the beautiful thought that he who is judge is also fellow-citizen, kinsman, brother, and above all Father.

The conviction that God is Father made the Jewish saints quite sure that forgiveness was always open to the penitent heart. Just as the parent will forgive the child who comes and says, " I'm sorry," so will God. " God says : I testify by heaven and earth that I sit and hope for Israel more than a father for his son or than a mother for her daughter, if only they would repent, so that my words could be fulfilled " (Tan.d.b. El. p.163). More than once the Jewish saints draw the picture of a prophet inviting the people to return in penitence to God, and of the people in the knowledge of their sin and their shame feeling the impossibility of even accepting the invitation. Then God says to them : " If you come back to me, is it not to your Father in Heaven that you come back? As

it is said, For I am a Father to Israel " (Jeremiah
31.9; Pes. K. 165a). There is another rabbinic passage
about a king's son who ran away. The king sent his
tutor to invite him to come back. "With what face
can I return?" said the son. "I am ashamed before
thee." And the father answered: "Can a son be
ashamed to return to his father?" And even so it is
with Israel and God (Deuteronomy R., Wa'ethanan
11.24). In passages like that there is a faith in God
which comes very close to the conception of God in
the parable of the Prodigal Son. Here is a picture of the
God who is the Father, and whose only desire is that
his wandering children should come home.

iii. But in spite of the beauty of the Jewish idea
of the fatherhood of God, the Jews never sentimentalised
the idea. They were quite clear that the fatherhood
of God involves the loving obedience of man. They
were very definite that the idea of God as a loving father
can never be used as an excuse for sinning; it must
rather be the summons to holy obedience. When
the prophets prayed to God to have mercy on his
children, God answered: "Only when they do my
will are they my children; when they do not do my
will they are not my children " (Exodus R. Ki Tissa xlvi,
4). "Hearken," says the rabbinic passage, "to thy
Father who is in heaven. He deals with thee as with
an only son, if thou obeyest him, but, if not, he deals
with thee as a slave. When thou doest his will he is
thy Father, and thou art his son, but if not, against
thy will, and opposed to thy consent, he is thine
owner and thou art his slave " (Pes. R. 132b). Here is
the idea that the will of God cannot in any event
be gainsaid. He who willingly and obediently accepts
it is the son of God; he who struggles against it has
in the end to accept it, not as a loving son, but as a

coerced slave, not as it were as a volunteer, but as a conscript. The Jewish saints allegorised the incident in Exodus 17.11 which tells how in the battle with Amalek Israel prevailed as long as Moses held up his hands but was defeated when Moses let his hands drop. "But could the hands of Moses promote the battle or hinder the battle? It is rather to teach you that such time as the Israelites directed their thoughts on high, and kept their hearts in subjection to their Father in heaven, they prevailed; otherwise they suffered defeat" (Rosh ha-Shanah 3.8). In the same way it was not looking at the fiery serpent that cured the man bitten by the serpents; it was the directing of the eyes and the thoughts on high to God the Father. How can a man "acquire God"? asks the Jewish preacher, and answers: "He may acquire him by his good deeds and by the study of the law" (Tan.d.b. El. p.128). The duty of the teacher of children is to teach children "to do the will of their Father who is in heaven." Rabbi Judah, the son of Tema, gave the beautiful command: "Be strong as a leopard, light as an eagle, fleet as a hart, and strong as a lion to do the will of thy Father who is in heaven" (Aboth v. 23).

The Jew always connected the thought of the loving and gracious fatherhood of God not with any kind of licence to sin, but with the absolute obligation to the response of loving obedience.

iv. We may note one last thing. The thought of the fatherhood of God laid upon the Jew the obligation to observe the brotherhood of man. Rabbi Jose said: "Why does God love widows and orphans? Because their eyes are turned to him, as it is said, A father of the fatherless, and a judge of the widows (Psalm 68.5). Therefore, anyone who robs them is as if he robbed God, their Father in heaven" (Exod. R. Mishpatim 30.8). If God is Father, then God will never look lightly on the man who injures or refuses to help one of his children.

Even before the Christian faith came into the world, and even before Jesus taught his men to pray " Our Father," there was in Jewish thought a great heritage of riches in the Jewish connection of the fatherhood of God. We now turn to study the new meaning and content which Jesus put into the phrase " Our Father " when it is addressed to God.

It is often easiest to see the sheer newness of some discovery of the mind of man, not in the first instance by looking at it, but by looking at the beliefs of men before the discovery was made, and at the beliefs of men, who after it was made disregarded it or refused to accept it. We will, therefore, best see the sheer newness of Jesus' idea of God by looking at men's ideas of God before he came into the world.

The two great pre-Christian philosophies by which men lived in the Graeco-Roman world were Stoicism and Epicureanism. For the Stoic the one essential attribute of God was *apatheia. Apatheia* in Greek is not apathy in the ordinary English sense of the term. In English apathy is the indifference of one who need not and should not feel indifferent. *Apatheia* in Greek is the essential inability to experience any feeling at all. The Greek argument was simple and logical. If a person can experience the feeling of joy or grief, or love or hate, it means that some other person can affect him. Some other person by his attitude can bring to him gladness or grief, can affect and change the feelings of his heart. Now to be able to affect another person is at least for the moment to have some kind of power over him. But clearly, as the Greeks saw it, no one can have any power over God. And the only way to ensure that this is so is to assume as a first principle that God, just because he is God, is entirely incapable of any feeling. He is *apathes,* passionless, emotionless, essentially indifferent.

For the Epicureans the supreme quality in life was *ataraxia,* by which they meant complete calm, perfect serenity. The Epicureans went on to argue that if God were involved in the affairs of the world, then his serenity would be gone for ever. So for him the essence of Godhead is complete and total detachment from the world. The gods may see the world, but they are completely detached from it. It is in fact precisely that serene unmoved detachment which makes them gods. Tennyson in the *Choric Song* in the *Lotos-Eaters* perfectly caught the Epicurean conception of the gods:

For they lie beside their nectar, and the bolts are
*   hurl'd*
Far below them in the valleys, and the clouds are
*   lightly curl'd*
Round their golden houses, girdled with the
*   gleaming world;*
Where they smile in secret, looking over wasted
*   lands,*
Blight and famine, plague and earthquake, roaring
*   deeps and fiery sands,*
Clanging fights, and flaming towns, and sinking
*   ships and praying hands.*

Here is the perfect picture of the Epicurean gods, insulated from all emotion and detached from all action and isolated from all interest.

Now let us take three pictures from the Old Testament. When we take these three pictures from the Old Testament, let us be quite clear what we are doing. We are not belittling the Old Testament; we are simply saying that the Old Testament thinkers did not know God as Jesus knew him. After all, if the Old Testament thinkers already perfectly knew God, there would have been no necessity for Jesus to come.

It was because men did not, and could not by themselves, know what God was like that God did come to
men in Jesus Christ.

First, let us take the great picture from Job 38 and 39.
These two chapters are supreme not only in the dramatic
poetry of the Old Testament but in the dramatic
poetry of the world. The Lord answers the tortured
and agonised Job out of the whirlwind. " Where were
you when I laid the foundations of the earth? Have
you commanded the morning since your days began?
Have you entered into the springs of the sea? Have
you comprehended the expanse of the earth? Have
you entered the storehouses of the snow? Can you
bind the chains of the Pleiades, or loose the cords of
Orion? Do you give the horse his might? Do you
clothe his neck with strength?" (Job 38.4, 12, 16, 18,
22, 31; 39.19). These chapters are the most awe-
inspiring divine bombardment of Job, and the whole
grim and terrible point of them is that God is saying
to Job: " What right have you to speak to me, or to
question me?" It would be difficult to imagine Jesus
speaking to any physically tortured and heart-broken
man like that.

Second, let us take Jeremiah's parable of the potter
(Jeremiah 18.1-11). Jeremiah saw the potter at work.
In the making of a vessel the vessel was marred, and
the potter simply wiped it out and began over again.
" Behold," Jeremiah takes God to say, " like the clay in
the potter's hand, so are you in my hand, O house of
Israel. Can I not do with you as the potter has done?"
(Jeremiah 18.6). Here is the picture of a God who will do
with living man what the potter does with soulless clay.
On this view man has no more rights in the eyes
of God than a lump of misshapen clay has in the
eyes of the potter. It is surely impossible to imagine
Jesus speaking of men as if they were *things*.

Third, let us take the picture of the Psalmist. In Psalm 24 the Psalmist lays down the conditions of approach to God as he sees them :

Who shall ascend the hill of the Lord?
   And who shall stand in his holy place?
He who has clean hands and a pure heart,
   who does not lift up his soul to what is false,
   and does not swear deceitfully.
He will receive blessing from the Lord,
   and vindication from the God of his salvation
                    (Psalm 24.3-5).

To anyone who thinks of the meaning of these words, apart from their poetry, they are terrible words, for, as he hears them, he hears the door to God slam in his face, for very certainly no human being can fulfil these conditions. It is impossible to conceive of the Jesus who said : " I came not to call the righteous, but sinners," speaking like that (Matthew 9.13).

Here are three Old Testament pictures of God which can only leave us terrified and afraid, and yet that is the way in which men thought of God before Jesus Christ.

Let us add to this three modern examples. James Stewart quotes two lines from a poem of Thomas Hardy and a saying of Voltaire. Thomas Hardy asks what can possibly be the use of prayer when we have no one to whom to pray except,

    The dreaming, dark, dumb Thing
    That turns the handle of the idle Show.

Voltaire's final verdict on life was, " A bad joke." " Ring down the curtain, the farce is done." H. G. Wells in one of his novels painted the picture of a man defeated by the stress and strain and tension of modern life. His doctor wisely told him that his only hope of re-taining his sanity was to find fellowship with God. " What?" said the man. " That—up there—having fellowship with me? I would as soon think of cooling my throat with the milky way or shaking hands with the stars."

Here then are the verdicts of those who do not know God in Jesus Christ. The Stoic sees his emotionless God; the Epicurean sees his utterly detached gods; the Old Testament writers paint in the most splendid but terrible terms the might and majesty and power and holiness of God; the modern writers can see nothing in God to which the man with the broken heart can appeal. And now let us turn to see something of that which Jesus put into this word father.

To begin with, we must look at the word *Father* itself. Great as it is, at first sight, to apply this word to God, it is still greater when we penetrate further into its meaning. In Gethsemane Jesus prayed, " Abba, Father " (Mark 14.36); and Paul twice writes to his people that we through the Holy Spirit can pray in the same way, and that we can use the same word as Jesus did when we too pray to God (Romans 8.15; Galatians 4.6). This word *abba* is more than *father*. It was the word by which a little child in Palestine addressed his father in the home circle as *jaba* still is in Arabic to-day. There is only one possible English translation of this word in any ordinary use of it, and that is " Daddy ". Of course, to translate it that way in the New Testament would sound bizarre and grotesque, but it does at once give us the atmosphere in which we come to God; we come to God with the simple trust and confidence with which a little child comes to a father whom he knows and loves and trusts. And Jeremias points out that there is no parallel in the whole of Jewish literature for the application of this word to God.

We would hardly need to go any further. Could there be any greater contrast to the Stoic *apatheia*, to the Epicurean detachment, to the Old Testament distance, to the modern doubt of the love of God, than this word *abba*? The plain fact is that no one in all the world had ever thought of God like that before, and to this day, apart from Jesus Christ, no one can think of God like this. The minute we use this word two things are settled straight away.

i. It settles once and for all *our relationship to God*. This is the spirit, this is the confidence, this is the intimacy with which we come to God.

When we go to Jesus' own words, we can still further fill out the meaning of this word.

a. First and foremost, it tells us that *God cares*. So far from being isolated, detached, insulated against all emotion, God cares for men with the constant love of a father, and with such a passion of love that in the end in Jesus Christ he suffered the agony of the Cross. The word has in it all the passion of the love of God.

b. Furthermore, we learn that this love of God is *a quite undeserved love*. Jesus cites it as typical of this fatherly love of God that God makes his sun to rise on the evil and the good and sends his rain on the just and the unjust (Matthew 5.45). This love of God is not kept for the good son and the son who never disobeys; it even reaches out to the son who goes his own way and breaks his father's heart and comes wretchedly home because he has nowhere else to go (Luke 15.11-32). There is no question of needing clean hands and a pure heart before we can enter into that love. God the Father loves us with a love which will never let us go.

c. And yet in spite of that *this love of God has its own rewards*. God in his own way, all unseen and all unknown, rewards the son who does his Father's will (Matthew 6.4,6,18). God has two kinds of sons, the sons who break his heart and the sons who delight

his heart, and there are precious things for those who
do their Father's will. The disobedient son is not shut
out, but there are things for the obedient son that the
disobedient son can never know, until he turns and
submits to his Father's love.

d. This fatherly love of God is a *practical love*. It
knows well that we need food and clothing and all
the necessary things of life. Our Father knows that we
need these things (Matthew 6.8, 32; Luke 12.30).
When we go to God in prayer, our prayers need not be
entirely " spiritual " and " religious ". We can pray
to God for our practical, worrying, every day needs.
There is nothing which we cannot take to God in
prayer.

e. So great is this love that it covers *the whole creation
of God*. God loves even the animals and the birds and
the flowers, every living thing his hands have made.
And the wonderful thing about this fatherhood of
God is that it is not only universal, as wide as the
world, it is *unbelievably detailed*. The same saying of
Jesus is reported differently in Matthew and in Luke.
In Matthew 10.29 it runs:

Are not two sparrows sold for a penny? And not
one of them will fall to the ground without your
Father's will.

In Luke 12.6 it runs:

Are not five sparrows sold for two pennies? And
not one of them is forgotten before God.

In Palestine a purchaser could buy two sparrows for one
penny; but if he was prepared to spend two pennies
he got, not four, but *five* sparrows. The extra sparrow
was thrown into the bargain; it was quite worthless; it
had no value at all; it mattered to no one; *but even
that extra sparrow matters to God.* Surely never did
Jesus say so clearly that there is no one who does not
matter in the sight of God.

Paul Tournier, the great Christian doctor, tells a tragic thing. In *A Doctor's Casebook* he writes : " There was one patient of mine, the youngest daughter in a large family, which the father found it difficult to support. One day she heard him mutter despairingly, referring to herself : 'We could well have done without that one !' " That is precisely what God can never say. In the same book Paul Tournier notes another thing. God says to Moses : " I know thee *by name* " (Exodus 33.17). He says to Cyrus : " I am the Lord, which call thee *by thy name* " (Isaiah 45.3). One of the features of the Bible is whole chapters of names, of genealogies. There was a time when Paul Tournier thought that these chapters could well have been omitted from the Bible, and then he came to see that they are the symbol of the infinite number of people whom God knows *by name*. The love of God is so detailed that the worthless sparrow matters to him, that there is no one whom he does not know by name. In point of fact the saying about the sparrow may be even more wonderful yet. " Not one of them will fall to the ground without your Father's will." We might think that that refers to the *death* of a sparrow. But my old teacher J. E. McFadyen used to love to suggest that, if we put that saying back into Aramaic, it may well mean, not that God sees it, if a sparrow *falls* to the ground, but if a sparrow *lights* on the ground. Every time the sparrow hops on the ground God sees it and knows.

Every time we pray, " Our Father," we can know for certain that for God no one is lost in the crowd; that if we matter to no one else, we matter to God; that if no one else cares for us, God cares. Here is something to lift up our hearts every time we pray our Lord's prayer.

ii. We began by saying that two things are settled by this address to God. It settles our relationship to

God; but equally it settles *our relationship to our fellow men*. The word before Father is *our*. The very use of that word ends all exclusiveness. If God is *our* Father, then our fellow man is our brother. The only possible basis for democracy is the conviction of the fatherhood of God. The only value that man possesses as man is that he is the child of God. Nationalism, racialism, snobbery, class distinction, the colour bar, *apartheid* stand uncompromisingly condemned in the two words which open our Lord's prayer. If we pray those words and hate or despise our brother man, then the prayer is a mockery and we make ourselves liars.

Our Father—we might almost say that a man need go no further than these two words in his prayers, for here once and for all there are settled our relationship to God and our relationship to our fellow men. Here are the two words which invite us to come into God's presence with childlike confidence and boldness and which forbid us to do anything but love any man.

HALLOWED BE THY NAME

It may well be that of all the petitions of the Lord's Prayer this prayer that God's name should be hallowed is the petition to which most people would find it most difficult to attach any definite and precise meaning, if they were asked what they meant when they were praying it. I once knew a small boy who always prayed it in a form all his own: "*Herald* be thy name"! And no doubt he was thinking of the "herald angels" of the Christmas hymn. Since this is so, we must begin with the basic task of establishing the meaning of the word in this petition.

Let us begin by tracing the various translations of this petition which different translators have offered. These translations fall into four groups.

i. There are the translations which use the word *hallowed*. This is the oldest translation of all. It goes back to Alfred the Great: "*Sic gehalyed dhin noma*"; and to Wicliffe: "Halewed be thy name". This word *hallowed* then came down to us via Tyndale, Coverdale, the Great Bible, the Geneva Bible, the Authorised Version, and the Revised Version. It is in the modern versions of Ronald A. Knox and of E. V. Rieu; and it is the word which is used in the New English Bible. From the first of the translations to the last this word *hallowed* is used. It has a long and honourable lineage, and even the most modern translators have felt that there was nothing better.

ii. There are the translations which use the word *holy*. Typical of them is Weymouth: "May thy name be kept holy." And in one form or another this is the translation of C. Kingsley Williams and of the Twentieth Century New Testament. It is the alternative translation of the Amplified New Testament : " Hallowed (kept holy) be your name." As we shall see, this translation is indeed very close to the original.

iii. There are the translations which use the word *sanctified*. Typical of this translation is the Douai-Rheims version : sanctified be thy name." This is also the word used by Schonfield in the Authentic New Testament. This translation is not really different, for in fact all that it does is to use the latinised form of the word *to hallow*.

iv. There are the translations which go, as we might say, a little further afield to find a rendering. Moffatt and Goodspeed uses the word *revered* : " Thy (your name be revered." Kenneth Wuest uses the word *venerated* : " Let your name be venerated." J. B. Phillips uses the word *honoured* : " May your name be honoured."

We may finally look at a translation which is not so much a translation as a curiosity. One of the most extraordinary of all modern translations is that of Edward Harwood, published in 1768 under the long title, *A Liberal translation of the New Testament: being an Attempt to translate the Sacred Writings with the same Freedom, Spirit and Elegance, with which other English Translations from the Greek Classics have lately been executed*. Harwood, whose translation F. F. Bruce not unfairly calls " a literary curio ", was perhaps the first of the paraphrasers, and his translation of the opening clauses of the Lord's Prayer, " Our Father which art in Heaven : Hallowed be thy name ", runs :

O Thou great governour and parent of universal nature—who manifestest thy glory to the blessed inhabitants of heaven—may all thy rational creatures in all the parts of thy boundless dominion be happy in the knowledge of thy existence and providence, and celebrate thy perfections in a manner most worthy thy nature and perfective of their own.

What Harwood is trying to do is clear enough, but whether or not he succeeded in doing it is quite another question!

Let us, then, turn to the definition of the meaning of the words in this petition and let us start with the meaning of the word *name*.

In biblical times the *name* stood for much more than the name by which a person is called in the modern sense of the term. The name stood for the whole character of the person as it was known, manifested, or revealed. As Origen puts it in commenting on this petition of the Lord's Prayer (*On Prayer* 24.2, 3) name is a term which summarises and manifests the personal character of him who is named. The name stands for " the personal and incommunicable character " of the person. The *name* of God, therefore, stands for the nature and the character and the personality of God as they have been revealed to men. This becomes quite clear when we see the way in which the *name* is used in Scripture. The Psalmist (Psalm 9.10) says:

Those who know thy name put their trust in thee.

That clearly does not mean that those who know God's name in the English sense of the term will willingly trust him; it means that those who know the character and nature and personality of God, those who know what God is like as he has revealed himself to be, will willingly trust in him. Again, the Psalmist (Psalm 20.7) says:

Some boast of chariots, and some of horses;
    but we boast of the name of the Lord our God.

That is to say, some regard chariots and horses as

their most powerful possessions, but to us the greatest
thing of all is the nature of God as he has revealed
himself to us. In John (17.6) Jesus says :

I have manifested thy name to the men whom thou
gavest me out of the world.

In effect, that means that Jesus clearly told his own
men *what God is like,* what the nature and the character
and the personality of God truly are. The name can
stand for nothing less than God himself. The Old
Testament can talk of " blaspheming the Name "—the
RSV prints *Name* with a capital letter—and that clearly
means insulting God himself. (Leviticus 24.16).

We begin, then, with the fact that the name means the
nature, the character, the personality of God as they
have been revealed to us.

We now move on to examine the meaning of the
word *hallow.* In Greek the word is *hagiazein,* which
is clearly connected with the word *hagios,* which is
generally translated *holy. Hagiazein* is practically non-
existent in secular Greek, but in biblical Greek there
is ample material to define its meaning. It has two
basic meanings. First, it means to make an ordinary
secular thing holy, by certain rituals or by bringing
it into contact with things which are holy. That is
obviously not the meaning here. Nothing that man
can do can make the name of God holy in that sense,
for that would imply that to start with the name of
God is *not* holy. But, second, *hagiazein* means to treat
as holy, that is, *to hold sacred.* To hallow a thing
is to regard and to treat that thing as holy and sacred.
But what does that mean? We can best come at this
from remembering the meaning of *hagios. Hagios* is
the adjective meaning *holy*; but the basic idea behind
it is the idea of *difference.* That which is *hagios* is
different from ordinary things; it belongs to a different
sphere of quality and of being. That is why God is

supremely The Holy One, for God supremely belongs to a different sphere of life and being.

This meaning becomes even clearer when we examine the word in use. The commandment is to remember the Sabbath day to keep it *holy* (Exodus 20.8). That is to say, the Sabbath day is to be regarded and to be kept as different from other days. The instruction is *to consecrate* the priest (Leviticus 21.8). This also is the word *hagiazein*, and clearly the meaning is to set the priest apart so that he is different from other and from ordinary men, so that, we might now say, he is different from *lay men*.

When we arrive at this stage, we can see that the meaning of the word *hagiazein* is beginning to acquire the meaning of *reverence*, for reverence is the characteristic attitude to that which is different, that which belongs to a sphere of being other than our own. There is an Old Testament passage (Numbers 20.1-11; cp. Deuteronomy 32.51) which well illustrates the meaning of this word. The story is that the children of Israel in their journeyings in the wilderness were near to perishing of thirst, and were full of bitter complaints. God instructed Moses to take his rod and to speak to the rock and to tell the rock to give forth water. But Moses, instead of only speaking to the rock, in his anger and irritation struck the rock. Then there comes the statement:

> Because you did not believe in me to *sanctify* me in the eyes of the people of Israel you shall not bring this assembly into the land which I have given them.

The verb *to sanctify* is *hagiazein;* Moffatt translates it, "because you did not vindicate my honour", and the Smith-Goodspeed translation is, "because you did not pay me my due honour". Basically, the idea is that the action of Moses was an action of *irreverence* in that it implied disobedience to God and distrust of God; by, as it were, taking the law into his own hands, Moses had been guilty of irreverence towards God.

So, then, we arrive at the conclusion that *to hallow* means *to reverence*. We have now defined the meaning of the two terms in this petition. The *name* of God is the character, nature and personality of God, as he has revealed them to us, in the Scriptures, in the world which he has made, and especially in Jesus Christ our Lord. *To hallow* is *to hold in reverence*. If we, then, pray, "Hallowed be thy name", the prayer means, "May you be given that unique reverence which your character and nature and personality, as you have revealed them to us, demand." The prayer is that God may be given that reverence which his divine being demands and necessitates, and which, through his self-revelation, we well know to be due to him. We get exactly the same idea in regard to Jesus in 1 Peter (3.15) where Peter bids his people: "Reverence (*hagiazein*) Christ as Lord." To Jesus there must be given the reverence which his lordship demands.

This conclusion is underlined by the fact that sometimes the Greek fathers use certain other words as the equivalent of *hagiazein*. Chrysostom equates it with *doxazein*, which means *to glorify* or *to honour*: Origen equates it with *hupsoun*, which means *to exalt* or *to lift on high*. And later *hagiazein* is often expressed by the word *eulogein*, which means to *bless* or *to praise*. To hallow God's name is to give God the reverence, the honour the glory, the praise, the exaltation which his character demands. Calvin puts it this way: "That God's name should be hallowed is nothing other than to say that God should have his own honour, of which he is worthy, so that men should never think or speak of him without the greatest veneration."

We have no sooner arrived at this conclusion than we

see at once that one possible threat and danger is removed. When we set down the relationship between
God and man that is involved in the word Father,
and especially in the word *Abba,* there must be in our
minds the awareness that it is possible for a certain
sentimentality to creep in. No doctrine is more liable
to be sentimentalised than the doctrine of the fatherhood
of God. But one thing becomes clear to anyone who
knows anything about Jewish religion and worship—
the fact that any such sentimentalisation is for a Jew
essentially impossible. For a Jew God is supremely The
Wholly Other; no Jew ever could think of God without
reverence.

One of the most interesting facts about Judaism is
that when a Jew called God Father he almost always
added to the word Father some other words which con-
served the majesty and the glory of God. So in Ecclesiasticus the prayer of the preacher is (Sir. 23.1):

O Lord, Father and Ruler of my life

and again (Sir. 23.4):

O Lord, Father and God of my life.

in 3 Maccabees (6.2-4) before the writer prays to God,
" O Father ", he has already prayed immediately before:

King of great power, most high, almighty God, who
governest all creation with loving-kindness.

In the greatest of all the Synagogue prayers, the
prayer known variously as the *Shermoneh 'Esreh,* that is,
the Eighteen Benedictions, or the *Amidah* prayer, or
the *Tefillah,* which means, as it were, the prayer *par
excellence,* the fifth and sixth Benedictions run:

Cause us to return, O our Father, to thy law,
and draw us near, O King, to thy service, and
restore us in perfect penitence to thy presence.
Blessed art thou, O Lord, who delightest in
repentance.

Forgive us, our Father, for we have sinned;

pardon us, our King, for we have transgressed;
ready to pardon and forgive thou art. Blessed art
thou, O Lord, most gracious, who dost abundantly
pardon.

Nothing is more characteristic of Jewish prayer than
the combination of the titles Father and King and Lord
in addresses to God.

In the *Ahabah rabbah* prayer which comes second
after the Shema (Jewish prayers are often known by
their opening words, and these words mean *with
abounding love*) there comes the petition:

Our Father, our King, for our fathers' sake who
trusted in thee, and whom thou didst teach the
statutes of life, be thou gracious to us likewise and
teach us.

In the famous *Kaddish* prayer which introduces the
various parts of the Synagogue service there is an
almost exact parallel to the first two clauses of the
Lord's Prayer:

Magnified and sanctified be his great name in the
world which he hath created according to his will.
May he establish his kingdom during your life
and during your days, and during the life of all
the house of Israel even speedily and at a near time,
and say ye Amen.

On the ten penitential days at the time of the Day of
Atonement the Jews pray the great *Abinu Malkenu*
(Our Father, our King) prayer. It has forty-four petitions all beginning, "Our Father, our King", of which
some are:

Our Father, our King, we have sinned before thee
Our Father, our King, we have none other King
but thee.
Our Father, our King, bring us back before thee
in perfect repentance.

Our Father, our King, vouchsafe to write us in the
Book of Redemption.

Our Father, our King, hear us, though no good
works of our own be in us.

We will sanctify also thy name throughout the
world, O God, the God of our fathers, reign
thou over the whole world in thy glory.

There may be a modern danger of sentimentalising
the idea of God as Father; it is not a danger into which
any Jew would ever have fallen. The Jews called
God Father, and loved to call him so, but they never
forgot that he was also the King and Lord of all the
earth. Reverence was never in any danger of being
obliterated by sentimentality.

So here in the Lord's Prayer we pray not only to our
Father, but to our *Father who is in heaven,* and then we
pray that God may receive the reverence which his
unique character and nature deserve and demand. We
have now to go on to see what in actual practice in
life it means to hallow the name of God, what it means
to give God that unique place which his nature and
character and personality demand. In other words,
we have to try to find out *what true reverence is.*

There is one basic prerequisite without which reverence
cannot even begin to exist. That prerequisite was perfectly stated by the writer to the Hebrews (11.6):
"Whoever would draw near to God must believe that
he exists and that he rewards those who seek him."
That is to say, there can be no such thing as reverence
without the twin basic beliefs, first, that God exists,
and, second, that God is interested in the attitude
and actions of men towards himself. The Bible itself
never seeks to prove the existence of God. In geometry
there are certain truths which are called axioms. Axioms
are not themselves proved; they are the basic truths
which are the foundation of all reasoning and of all

proofs. For the biblical writers God is an axiom, more, God is *the* axiom, the fact of whose existence is the basic fact of life. The biblical writers would have said that they no more needed to prove the existence of God than they needed to prove the existence of their wife or of their closest friend. They did not need to prove the existence of God, because they daily met God; they did not need to argue about God, because they daily and hourly met God. As for the fact that God is interested in man's response and reaction to himself, to the Christian thinker there is no need to go beyond the incarnation to find proof of that. The interest of God in men is such that he in Jesus Christ entered into life to bring men to himself. The Christian can never have any doubt that God " exists and that he rewards those who seek him."

How, then, shall we express this reverence for the God who exists and the God who is interested in us? Tholuck finds that the commentators on this petition interpret its obligation in three different ways.

i. They interpret it, as we might say, from the negative angle, and take it to mean that God's name should never be profaned but always named with reverence. This is obviously a narrow interpretation, and has to do with a man's speaking and nothing else.

ii. They interpret it more positively to mean that God must be praised and glorified in words. This would mean that we hallow the name of God and that we reverence him in the prayers and praises of the liturgy and in the acts of worship in the narrower sense of the term. This is still a narrow interpretation, and confines this necessary reverence to the worship men offer within the Church.

iii. They interpret it to mean that God must be reverenced in the heart, and that our outward walk and conversation should continually show this inward reverence, since from such a life others too are moved to reverence God. This in effect means that we must reverence God and hallow the name of God in the actions of everyday life.

There is no doubt which is the correct interpretation. The reverence which is demanded cannot be confined to words; it cannot be confined to the liturgy and praises of the Church, however splendid they may be; it must be lived and demonstrated in every moment of our lives, both in the Church and in the world. We find in the early fathers specially illuminating interpretations of this petition, and always along these lines. They see this reverence exemplified in three directions.

i. We reverence God *when our beliefs concerning God are such as are worthy of God*. That is to say true doctrine and true teaching are reverence for God; false doctrine and false teaching are irreverence to God. Origen (*On Prayer* 24) brings this out. God has revealed himself as HE WHO IS (Exodus 3.14). Now everyone makes his own suppositions about God; everyone knows something about God; but man being man can only grasp a very little of the holiness of God. And, because we are so liable to make mistakes, and to confuse partial truths with the whole truth, we are taught to pray " that our concept of God may be hallowed amongst us ". " The man who brings into his concept of God ideas which have no place there takes the name of the Lord God in vain." Since *the name* of God means *the nature* and *the character* of God, anyone who brings into his idea of God thoughts and conceptions which are alien to the true character of God is guilty of irreverence and of failure to hallow the name of God.

To take the obvious example, the Greeks with their stories of the wars and battles and struggles and quarrels, the loves and hates and seductions and adulteries of the gods, were in fact guilty of irreverence, for they were bringing into the conception of God things which had no right to be there. But Christians themselves have been far from guiltless in this matter. Very often men have been repelled by ideas of God which show God as savage, vindictive, harsh and cruel, and the very opposite of the God whom we see in Jesus Christ. There will be those who will not agree, but it may well be that those who presented men with the conception of a God who banned unbaptised children from heaven and who predestined one man to heaven and another to hell for his own glory have been guilty of the sin of irreverence. There have been times when God has been presented as a God of battles and a kind of nationalistic ally. There have been times when men have drawn a picture of God to suit their own theories of racial superiority. There have been times when men used their own ideas of God to erect a barrier to all social progress, and when they did indeed make religion the opiate of the people, when they made religion an argument for maintaining the *status quo*. There have been theories of the Atonement which at least by implication set over against each other a God of avenging justice and a Christ of sacrificial love. John Wesley was right when he said of one who had such beliefs: "Your God is my devil."

To allow into our conception of God things which are unworthy of God, and things which can have no place in the God who is the God and Father of our Lord Jesus Christ is to fail to hallow the name of God; it is to be guilty of irreverence, and, worst of all, it has been the reason why countless thousands of men and women have been repelled by the Church and its teaching. If we are to hallow God's name, we must see to it that our conception of God is truly Christian.

ii. We reverence God and we hallow God's name,

when our life is such that it brings honour to God and attracts others to him. This is an idea to which the early fathers return again and again. Cyril of Jerusalem (*Catechetical Lecture* 23) begins by saying that quite clearly God's name is in itself and in its nature holy, no matter what we may say or do, or not say or not do. The prayer cannot possibly mean that God's name should become holy from not being holy. We are to pray this prayer because God's name "becomes holy in us, when we are made holy, and do things worthy of holiness." Cyprian (*On the Lord's Prayer* 12) says that it is obviously impossible that we should wish for God that he should be hallowed by our prayer; what we do ask is that "his name should be hallowed in us." Tertullian (*On Prayer* 3) says exactly the same thing. The prayer is that "God's name may be hallowed in us." Augustine (*The Sermon on the Mount* 5.19) makes exactly the same point. It is not that God's name is not already holy. What we do pray for is that men should regard it as holy, that is to say, that God may become so near and dear to us that we will esteem nothing more holy than his name and dread nothing more than to offend it.

This is worked out most fully and most relevantly by Gregory of Nyssa in his third Sermon on the Lord's Prayer. We pray this prayer because in itself human nature is too weak to achieve any of the things which it well knows it ought to achieve. The good can only be accomplished in us by divine aid. And of all good things the most important for us is *that God should be glorified through our lives.* This, says Gregory, will become quite clear, if we look at it from the negative angle first. Paul condemns those (Romans 2.24) through whom God has to say: "The name of God is blasphemed among the Gentiles." The Christian is living in a pagan environment; and, if the heathen see the

Christian living an immoral, an irreligious and an unlovely life, they attribute the ugliness of that life not
to the fault of the individual Christian, but to the
Christianity of which the individual Christian is the
sample and representative. Not the Christian but Christianity is blamed for such conduct. The prayer really
means : " Let the name of God be hallowed *in me,* so
that men may see our good works and glorify our Father
who is in heaven." Any reasonable man will in honesty
be compelled to glorify God " if he sees in those who
believe in him a life firmly established in virtue . . .
purged from all sin, above any suspicion of evil, and
shining with temperance and holy prudence."

Then Gregory goes on to describe the kind of life which
the man who in his life hallows the name of God will
live : " A man who leads such a life will oppose for-
titude to the assaults of the passions; since he partakes
of the requirements of life only as far as is necessary,
he is in no way softened by the luxuries of the body and
is an utter stranger to revelry and laziness as well
as to boastful conceit. He touches the earth but lightly
with the tip of his toes, for he is not engulfed by the
pleasurable enjoyments of its life, but is above all
deceit that comes by the senses. And so, even although
in the flesh, he strives after the immaterial life. He
counts the possession of virtues the only riches, familiarity with God the only nobility. His only privilege and
power is the mastery of self so as not to be a slave
to human passions. He is saddened if his life in this
material world be prolonged; like those who are sea-
sick he hastens to reach the port of rest." He goes on
to say that, when he prays this petition, what he is
really praying is : " May I become through thy help
blameless, just and pious, may I abstain from every
evil, speak the truth, and do justice. May I walk in
the straight path, shining with temperance, adorned

with incorruption, beautiful through wisdom and prudence. May I meditate upon the things that are above and despise what is earthly, showing the angelic way of life. . . . For a man can glorify God in no other way save by his virtue which bears witness that the Divine Power is the cause of his goodness."

Here in truth this petition is driven home to us. The name of God can only be hallowed when every action of our life is a witness to our faith in him, and when we continuously bring credit to the name we bear. The early fathers stress this with such intensity because they were living in a pagan environment, and the only way in which Christianity could spread and could conquer the world was by the individual Christian living a life of such beauty and goodness and truth that others might wish to share the secret of that loveliness. The one thing which was fatal was a life which brought the Christian faith and the Christian Church into disrepute. The plain fact is that the situation has not changed. It may be that we do not now live in a society which is hostile to Christianity; we live in a society in which Christianity and the Church have become irrelevant. And, if the Christian is just as likely to collapse under sorrow, if his life is just as frustrated and unsatisfied as the life of the non-Christian, if he is just as worried and anxious, just as nervous and restless, just as guilty of petty dishonesty, of self-seeking, of measuring everything by material values as the man who makes no profession of Christianity, then quite clearly no one will want Christianity because the obvious conclusion is that it makes no difference anyway. Nietzsche, the famous German pagan philosopher, said a thing which flings the challenge at every professing Christian : " Show me that you are redeemed and then I will believe in your redeemer." The very essence of this petition is that in it we pray that God may enable us to show that we are redeemed, so that in our lives he may be glorified, and so that through us others may come to desire the secret which we possess. This petition prays that we may be enabled so to show Christ to men that men may desire Christ.

iii. It is quite clear that this petition represents not only a prayer on our part, but also a demand on the part of God, a demand which without God's help we cannot fulfil. If, then, we are to hallow the name of God, we must first of all enthrone God within our hearts. In his commentary on this petition Origen (*On Prayer* 24.4) has a lovely, if maybe far-fetched, piece of exegesis. He identifies *hallowing* the name of God with *extolling* the name of God. He then quotes Psalm 30.1 : "I will extol thee, O Lord, for thou hast drawn me up, and hast not let my foes rejoice over me." In this Psalm the Psalmist *extols, hallows,* the name of God. Then Origen goes on to quote the title at the head of this Psalm : "A Psalm of David. A Song at the Dedication of the Temple." Then he draws his deduction : "We extol God when we dedicate within ourselves a house to God." To extol God, to hallow God's name, must in the last analysis mean that we make our hearts his temple and his dwelling-place, for only when he dwells within our hearts will our lives truly honour him and truly draw others to him.

Hallowed be thy name—here is the petition which saves the idea of the Fatherhood of God from all sentimentality and which sets down in unmistakable terms the inescapable obligation of reverence. In it we pray that God himself should enable us to give to him the unique place which his nature and character and personality as revealed in Jesus Christ demand and deserve. And we give him that place only when our conception of him is truly Christian and has no dregs of unlovely unworthiness in it, and when our lives are so clothed with the beauty of holiness that they are a continual invitation to share the secret which we possess in Jesus Christ. And we know that we can never do that until we enthrone him as King within our hearts.

In his Larger Catechism Martin Luther asks the question: "How is it (God's name) hallowed amongst us?" And he gives the answer: "When our life and doctrine are truly Christian." So, then, this petition is at one and the same time a challenge to Christian action and an invitation to Christian commitment.

THY KINGDOM COME

It would be both possible and natural to hold that "Thy Kingdom come" is the central petition of the Lord's Prayer, for it is quite certain that the Kingdom of God was the central message and proclamation of Jesus. When Mark tells how Jesus first publicly emerged upon the scene, he summarises the message of Jesus: "The time is fulfilled, and the Kingdom of God is at hand; repent, and believe in the gospel" (Mark 1.14; cp. Matthew 4.17). Luke tells how Jesus told his disciples that they must be moving on. "I must preach the good news of the Kingdom of God to the other cities also, for I was sent for this purpose" (Luke 4.43). The announcement of the Kingdom was nothing less than the purpose for which Jesus came into the world. The centrality of the idea of the Kingdom is made clear from the fact that the phrase the Kingdom of God, or the Kingdom of Heaven, appears 49 times in Matthew, 16 times in Mark and 38 times in Luke.

It is quite clear that, if this idea is so central to the message of Jesus, we must clearly understand what the Kingdom is, and what its relevance is to us, before we can genuinely pray this prayer. There are two quite general facts that we must first note.

i. It might be better to talk of the *kingship* or of the *reign* of God. In modern speech the word *kingdom* is apt to mean a certain territory or area of land, as, for instance, when we speak of the kingdom of Belgium or the kingdom of Holland, or the kingdom of Great

Britain and Ireland. But in the New Testament the kingdom is not a territory; it is the reign of God. "The Kingdom of God is at hand" means "God is on the point of beginning his reign; the kingship, the royal power, of God within the world, is about to begin."

ii. The New Testament uses two phrases, the Kingdom of God and the Kingdom of Heaven. The two phrases mean exactly the same and it is an error to try to make any distinction between them. The facts are that Matthew hardly ever speaks of the Kingdom of God and practically always speaks of the Kingdom of Heaven, while Mark and Luke practically never speak of the Kingdom of Heaven and always speak of the Kingdom of God. The reason for that variation in practice is this. A devout Jew was very hesitant to take the name of God upon his lips at all. If it was possible he would always use some reverential periphrasis. The obvious periphrasis for God is heaven. Matthew is the most Jewish of the Gospel writers, and to avoid using the name of God he speaks rather of the Kingdom of Heaven, while Mark and Luke, being much less influenced by Jewish background, do not hesitate to speak of the Kingdom of God.

One of the most curious facts of the Gospels is that there is no definition of the Kingdom. The Kingdom is described in pictures and in analogies and in its demands and effects, but it is never in so many words defined. If we are to discuss it, we must have a working definition of it. Hebrew literary style is marked by the continuous use of parallelism. It is the common Hebrew practice to say everything twice; and the second arm of the parallel restates, or amplifies, or explains the first. This Hebrew characteristic is exemplified best of all in almost every verse of the Psalms.

The Lord of hosts is with us;
The God of Jacob is our refuge
                    (Psalm 46.7).
The Lord is thy keeper;
The Lord is thy shade on thy right hand
                    (Psalm 121.5).

In the Lord's Prayer two petitions appear side by side :

Thy Kingdom come;
Thy will be done in earth as it is in heaven
                    (Matthew 6.10).

If we may assume that here there is an instance of normal Hebrew parallelism, and that the second arm of the parallel explains and defines the first, then we can arrive at the definition : The Kingdom of God is a society upon earth in which God's will is as perfectly done as it is in heaven. That is to say, to do the will of God and to be in the Kingdom are one and the same thing. To be a citizen of any kingdom, and to be a subject of any king, necessarily involve obedience to the laws of that kingdom and to the commands of that king. To be a member of the Kingdom of God necessarily involves acceptance of the will of God.

This at once explains Jesus' place in the Kingdom, and it also explains certain puzzling New Testament sayings. In Matthew 11.11 Jesus is reported as saying : "Truly I say to you, among those born of women there has arisen no one greater than John the Baptist; yet he who is least in the Kingdom of Heaven is greater than he " (cp. Luke 7.28). The implication is that with the coming of Jesus and the coming of the Kingdom something completely new entered into life. What is that new thing? Let us remember our definition of the Kingdom; to be in the Kingdom means the perfect acceptance and the perfect performance of the will of God. Jesus Christ was the one and only person who ever fully accepted and fully carried out the will of God. *Therefore with Jesus the Kingdom came.* In him the Kingdom arrived. He incarnates and embodies the Kingdom. Jesus not only *proclaimed* the Kingdom; he *is* the Kingdom demonstrated in human life. He brought to men the message and the manifestation of the Kingdom.

Immediately we see the Kingdom in terms of the will of God, the Kingdom becomes *a personal thing.* The Kingdom of God is not something which in the first place involves nations and peoples and countries. *The Kingdom of God is something which begins with me.* To speak of the Kingdom is not to state a theological doctrine; it is not to institute a political programme; it is to confront oneself with a personal challenge in which we either accept or refuse the will of God for us. The Chinese Christian wisely prayed : " Lord, revive thy Church, beginning with me "; the Christian may equally wisely pray : " Lord, bring in thy Kingdom, beginning with me." The Kingdom involves the individual acceptance of the will of God. Therefore, to pray, " Thy Kingdom come," is to pray, " Lord, help me to do your will."

This is made even clearer when we look at two parallel New Testament passages. In Mark 9.43 we read :

If your hand causes you to sin, cut it off; it is better for you *to enter into life* maimed than with two hands to go to hell.

In Mark 9.47 we read :

If your eye causes you to sin, pluck it out; it is better for you *to enter the Kingdom of Go*d with one eye than with two eyes to be thrown into hell.

In these two passages *life* and *the Kingdom* are one and
the same thing. We only find life in obedience to God.
In doing his will we find our peace. Only in the
Kingdom is there life, because clearly life is what
it was meant to be only when it is lived in obedience
to the will of God.

When we realise the indissoluble connection between
the Kingdom and the will of God and life, then a whole
series of New Testament passages and pictures and
ideas fall into place.

i. In view of this it is entirely natural that the
Kingdom of God should *begin with an invitation.* It
begins with the personal invitation of God to every
man to accept his will, as that will is known in Jesus
Christ. It may therefore be pictured as a feast and a
banquet to which the host issues invitations, which the
guests can accept or refuse to their glory or their
shame (Matthew 22.1-14; Luke 14.16-24). To enter
the Kingdom is to accept the invitation of God to be
his guest, and a guest must always accept the laws
and rules of the family into which he enters.

ii. This is why *the Kingdom of God and repentance
go hand in hand.* The initial message of Jesus was
a summons to repent because God was about to begin
his reign (Mark 1.14; Matthew 4.17). Repentance is
literally *a change of mind (metanoia)*; and conversion
is literally *a turning round and a facing in the opposite
direction.* The instinctive human relationship to life is
to make our own will, wishes and desires the dominat-
ing and moving force in life. When a man enters
the Kingdom he has that change of mind which makes
him stop obeying his own will and begin accepting
God's will, which makes him stop looking at himself
and start looking at God. A Christian is a man who
has accepted the fact that he can never again do what
he likes; and that he must for ever after do what

God likes. The Christian life begins for a man, the entry to the Kingdom begins for him, when like Paul on the Damascus road, his one question is : "What shall I do, Lord?" (Acts 22.10).

iii. This is why the Kingdom of God necessarily *starts from the smallest beginnings*. Men do not enter the Kingdom in crowds; they must enter as individuals; for the moment of entry is the personal and individual acceptance of the will of God. That is why the growth of the mustard seed, the smallest of all seeds, into a tree symbolises the Kingdom (Matthew 13.31, 32). That is why, if a man is placed in an environment which is hostile or indifferent to the claims of God, he must not regard it as something to regret and resent, but as a privilege and a challenge to be the tiny seed from which the Kingdom grows.

iv. This explains why a man can be *not far from the Kingdom*. Jesus told the wise and instructed Scribe that he was not far from the Kingdom (Mark 12.28-34). A man can be in a position when he knows the will of God, and when he at least partly desires to accept it, but when he trembles on the brink of the great submission. And that is exactly why one of the barriers to the Kingdom is the inability to make a clear-cut decision. "No one," said Jesus to the would-be follower, "who puts his hand to the plough and looks back is fit for the Kingdom of God" (Luke 9.61, 62). There cannot be anything like a benevolent neutrality to the Kingdom of God. We may be on the very brink of it, but we cannot be in it until we make what may even be the surgical decision to accept the will of God.

v. This explains why the situation which the challenge of the Kingdom creates is *necessarily a mixture*. More than one parable of Jesus makes exactly that point. The wheat and the tares grow together (Matthew

13.24-30). The dragnet brings in all sorts of things (Matthew 13.47). If the entry to the Kingdom and the acceptance of the will of God are one and the same, then there can be all sorts of reactions to the demand of the Kingdom. There may be blunt and deliberate rejection of the will of God. There may be a wistful yearning to accept it and yet an inability to make the necessary submission. There may be different levels of acceptance ranging from a tentative and timorous acceptance of the will of God to a gallant and adventurous total commitment to it. The mixture of the human situation is something which is inherent in the human situation in its relationship to God and his will.

vi. It is exactly here that there lies *the difference* in the idea of the Kingdom which Jesus brought to men. "My kingship," said Jesus to Pilate, "is not of this world" (John 18.36). The Jews saw the Kingdom in terms of material prosperity, in terms of political power, in terms of national greatness. In the Kingdom of God they expected the world to be luxuriant with new beauty and new plenty; they expected the Jews at last to take their place in world leadership. To this day it is not uncommon to interpret the Kingdom in terms of social reform and material blessings. True, these things are part of the Kingdom, but they are the *end* not the *beginning* of the Kingdom; they are not so much the Kingdom itself as the results of the Kingdom. "My Kingdom is within (or, among) you," Jesus said (Luke 17.21). Jesus was quite clear that the initial change must come in people, for, if it did not, any new situation would simply relapse into the old all over again. The different demand that Jesus made was that the individual person must accept the will of God before there could be any change in society at all. The Kingdom must come in the hearts of men before the Kingdom could even begin to come in the world at large.

There is still much to say about the individual and the Kingdom, but we have arrived at the basic truth that to be in the Kingdom and to accept and do the will of God are one and the same thing, and they are the only thing which leads to life as God meant it to be. It is in light of this basic truth that we must understand a group of sayings of Jesus which stress the intensity of the effort necessary to enter the Kingdom.

i. To enter the Kingdom of God is *worth any effort*. Jesus said: " Seek first his Kingdom and his righteousness " (Matthew 6.33), and this has been well translated: "Make the Kingdom of God the object of all your endeavour." Luke and Matthew both have their own versions of a difficult saying of Jesus. In Luke 16.16 we read: " The Law and the prophets were until John; since then the good news of the Kingdom of God is preached, and everyone enters it violently (AV, everyone presseth into it)." The word used for *entering violently* or *pressing into* is *biazesthai*, which is the word used of an army storming a city in a desperate attempt to gain an entry. Matthew repeats this saying: "From the days of John the Baptist until now the Kingdom of Heaven has suffered violence, and men of violence take it by force" (Matthew 11.12). It is possible, especially in its Matthew version, that this saying refers to the violent persecution and attack that the Kingdom has suffered; but it is more likely, especially in its Luke version, that this saying has the idea of men storming their way into the Kingdom as valorous troops would storm their way into a city. "The Kingdom of Heaven," Denny somewhere writes, " is not for the well-meaning but for the desperate." The dilettante Christian will never gain entry into the Kingdom. The Kingdom is for those who are desperately in earnest. We need look no further than the tragic drama of Gethsemane to see how hard it was even for Jesus to accept the will of God and to act on it. Quite simply the meaning is : It is worth any effort, it is worth any agony, it is worth any blood and sweat and tears to do the will of God, and therefore to be a citizen and member of the Kingdom.

ii. The Kingdom of God is worth *any price*. Jesus told the twin parables of the treasure hid in the field and the pearl of great price (Matthew 13. 44-46). In both cases the discoverer of the treasure gave his all to become the possessor of the treasure. It may well be that in order to become a member of the Kingdom and in order to do the will of God a man may have to pay a costly price. He may have to sacrifice an ease and comfort that he might have enjoyed. He may have to lay aside a personal ambition which he might well have attained. He may have to sacrifice even the nearest and dearest personal relationships, for Jesus demanded that loyalty to him should exceed even the loyalties to kith and kin which are at the very heart of human life (Matthew 10.37; Luke 14.26). The meaning is that there is no price too high to pay to be a member of the Kingdom and to do the will of God.

iii. To enter the Kingdom of God is worth *any sacrifice*. The hand, the eye, the foot which are liable to become a cause of sin have to be torn out and cut off and thrown away (Matthew 10.29, 30). No sacrifice is too radical and too surgical to make, if it is the price of entering the Kingdom and doing the will of God.

Before we leave this side of the matter, there are certain things to be said.

This is the necessary corrective to the idea that the

only kind of Christianity is that kind of Christianity which is pictured as serenely and unquestioningly accepting the will of God. If Christianity must be like that, then in all reverence we must say that Jesus Christ did not possess it, for Jesus Christ sweated blood in the Garden in the agony of the battle to accept the will of God. There is little credit in doing that which is no effort to do or in winning a bloodless victory against a phantom enemy. Let no man be ashamed when he has to battle terribly to accept the will of God for himself; he is walking the way his Master trod. The shame is not in the battle, but in losing the battle.

But it remains to be said in this matter that God will be in no man's debt. If the battle is bitter, the reward of victory is great. Whatever sacrifice a man makes, it will be repaid to him a hundredfold (Luke 18.29; Mark 10.28-30; Matthew 19.27-30). The struggle is not for nothing and therefore it can be faced with gallantry and joy.

We now turn to the qualifications which fit a man to enter the Kingdom. To begin with we find two such qualifications in the Beatitudes.

i. The Kingdom and its blessings belong to *the poor in spirit* (Matthew 5.3). In Greek the word is *ptochos*, and it means, not only *poor*, but absolutely and completely *destitute*. It translates the Hebrew word *ani*, which describes the poor, humble man, who in his helplessness and his trouble has put his whole trust in God. This then means that the Kingdom belongs to those who have recognised their own total destitution and who have put their whole trust in God. Entry to the Kingdom belongs to the man who humbly rests his poverty in God's wealth, his ignorance in God's wisdom, his sin in God's mercy, his moral failure and his battle with temptation in God's grace. It belongs to the man who recognises the obligation to do the will of God, but who also recognises his utter inability to do it without the help that God can give.

ii. The Kingdom and its blessings belong to those who are persecuted for righteousness' sake (Matthew 5.10). The persecuted are clearly those who love God's will more than personal comfort, personal reputation, personal ambition, personal safety and security, more than even life itself. The threat which obedience to God will nowadays bring to most people is not that of the loss of life and liberty. But it may well be the threat of unpopularity, ridicule, loneliness, sacrifice for principle. H. G. Wells once said that the characteristic of this age was that in it the voice of our neighbour is for many of us far louder than the voice of God. For the man who would enter the Kingdom the voice of God must be the most compelling thing in the universe.

iii. More than once Jesus lays it down that one of the supreme conditions of entry to the Kingdom is the possession of the childlike spirit (Matthew 18.2, 3; Mark 10.14, 15; Matthew 19.14; Luke 18.16, 17). The child has two great qualities—humility and trust. A normal child does not want prominence, place and prestige. A normal child never doubts that his home will be there waiting for him; he will set out on a journey with his parents on which he does not know the way and on which he can pay for nothing in perfect trust. Humility and trust are the passports to the Kingdom.

iv. There is a puzzling passage in the Sermons on the Mount in Matthew 5.17-20. There Jesus stresses the Law; not a letter and not the smallest part of a letter of it will ever become invalid. Anyone who relaxes its demands has but a low place in the Kingdom. " I tell you, unless your righteousness exceeds that of the Scribes and Pharisees, you will never enter the Kingdom of Heaven." What is the meaning of this?

The meaning is that he who enters into membership of the Kingdom is on a harder assignment than ever a Scribe or a Pharisee was. The Scribes and the Pharisees based life on the obedience to law. Now the very characteristic of law is that it is possible to satisfy it. When a man has done that which the law requires, when he has paid his just and lawful debts, when he has tholed his assize, in the Scots phrase, when he has stood his trial and paid his penalty, the law has no more claim on him. But the characteristic of life in the Kingdom is that its law is love, and the characteristic of love is that no man can ever satisfy its demands. No man has ever loved unless he has felt that, even if he gave his loved one the sun and the moon and the stars, it would not be enough. To be loved is to be placed in a debt which it is beyond the wit and power of man ever to pay. The obligation that is laid on the Christian is an obligation that no Scribe or Pharisee ever even glimpsed. The law of the Kingdom is love, and therefore the responsibility of the member of the Kingdom to God and to his fellowmen is without limit.

Just as there are certain qualifications of entry to the Kingdom, there are also certain barriers to entry to the Kingdom.

i. *Lip service* debars a man from entry to the Kingdom. It is not the man who says Lord, Lord, who will enter the Kingdom but the man who does the will of God (Matthew 7.21). Profession without practice is maybe one of the commonest of all faults within the Church. One of the prayers written for the Lambeth Conference of 1948 runs as follows:

Almighty God, give us grace to be not only hearers but doers of thy holy word, not only to admire but to obey thy doctrine, not only to profess but to practise thy religion, not only to love but to live thy gospel. So grant that what we learn of thy glory we may receive into our hearts and show forth in our lives.

That indeed is the way to the Kingdom.

ii. *The unforgiving spirit* debars a man from the Kingdom. Jesus makes this quite clear in the parable of the unforgiving debtor (Matthew 18.23-35). A merciless man can have no fellowship with the merciful God. A heart of hatred has automatically shut itself to the love of God. A man who will not forgive cannot enter into the presence of the God whose one desire it is to forgive. He who would be forgiven must learn to forgive. There is no place in the Kingdom for any man who in his heart nourishes a grudge against a fellowman and who in his life has an unhealed breach between himself and another.

iii. *Riches* make entry into the Kingdom very difficult. Jesus said : " Truly I say to you, it will be hard for a rich man to enter the Kingdom of Heaven. Again I tell you, it is easier for a camel to go through the eye of a needle than for a rich man to enter the Kingdom of God " (Matthew 19.23, 24; Mark 10.23-27; Luke 18.24, 25). Why? There are two main reasons.

First, the possession of many material things tends to fix a man's interests and thoughts to this world. He has so large a stake in this world that he can scarcely lift his eyes beyond it. Dr. Johnson made his famous remark to Boswell after leaving the castle and policies of a great nobleman : " Ah, Boswell, these are the things which make it difficult to die." It is possible for a man to get so involved in this world that he forgets that there is any other.

Second, riches can become what some one has called " a rival salvation ". They tend to give a false sense of security; they tend to make a man think that he can buy his way into and out of anything. They tend to make a man think that he can very well cope with life himself, and to make him forget God.

Jesus never said that riches debarred a man from the Kingdom, but he did say that they made entry to the Kingdom very difficult, for they tend to make a man forget that there is a Kingdom.

We may gather together, finally, certain remaining facts about the Kingdom.

The Kingdom involves the defeat of suffering, disease and death (Matthew 4.23; 10.1, 7, 8; 11.1-6; Mark 6.7; Luke 7.19-23; 9.11). It was Jesus' claim that if by the finger of God he cast out devils, the Kingdom had come (Matthew 12.28). The Kingdom of God is necessarily the defeat of evil and its power.

The Kingdom is universal. The gospel of the Kingdom will be preached in all the world (Matthew 24.14), and they will come from the north and the south and the east and the west to sit down in the Kingdom (Matthew 8.11; Luke 13.29). There are no racial distinctions, there are no most favoured nations, there are no *herrenvolk* in the Kingdom of God.

The Kingdom of God will come. Secretly, silently, but unstoppably the seed grows (Mark 4.26-29). Man can delay the Kingdom and man can hinder the Kingdom, but in the end the Kingdom will come.

The growth is not a growth which is infinite and unending; it is a growth which moves to a consummation. The Kingdom begins in time, but it has an end when eternity will finally break in upon time and when the kingdoms of the world will become the Kingdom of the Lord and of his Christ.

Thy Kingdom come—what a petition this is! It is not simply a petition that something will happen to the world of which we as it were will be spectators. It is a prayer that we should accept the will of God; that we should pay the price of that acceptance; that we should cleanse life of all that hinders that acceptance; that we should get to ourselves the things which are the passports to the Kingdom. No man need pray this prayer unless he is prepared to hand himself over to the grace of God in order that that grace may make him a new creature. This is no prayer for the man who desires to stay the way he is.

THY WILL BE DONE

It might well be said that "Thy will be done" is not only one of the petitions that Jesus taught his disciples to pray, but that it is also the centre, the key-note, and the ruling principle of Jesus' own life. Especially in the Fourth Gospel Jesus is represented as the One who came into the world for no other purpose than to do the will of God.

The disciples left Jesus tired at the well of Sychar in Samaria to go into the village to buy food. When they returned, they found that he did not wish to eat. They wondered if some one else had brought him food, but he said to them: "My food is to do the will of him who sent me, and to accomplish his work" (John 4.31-34). "I seek not my own will," he said, "but the will of him who sent me" (John 5.30). "I have come down from heaven," he said, "not to do my own will, but the will of him who sent me" (John 6.38). And this reaches its unsurpassable peak in Gethsemane, where Jesus ends his prayer with the words of perfect submission: "Nevertheless, not as I will, but as thou wilt" (Matthew 26.39). "Thy will be done" (Matthew 26.42). But to this we will return.

Such an attitude to life is wholly in keeping with all that was highest and best in Jewish religion. The greatest thing in all the world for the Jew was the *Torah*, the Law, the instruction of God. Clearly, the obverse of law is obedience; and for a Jew life's greatest duty and life's greatest privilege was obedience to the Law. And it must always be remembered that the Jewish attitude to the Law was not the attitude of one who obeys because he is afraid of the consequences if he does not; it was not the attitude of one to whom obedience is a wearisome and burdensome and irksome obligation and necessity; it was the attitude of the lover whose greatest joy on earth it is to seek to obey the least behest of his loved one.

We have, for instance, only to read Psalm 119 to see the Jew's throbbing delight in obedience to God. "Make me to understand the way of thy precepts . . . I have chosen the way of faithfulness; I set thy ordinances before me . . . I will run in the way of thy commandments . . . Teach me, O Lord, the way of thy statutes; and I will keep it to the end" (verses 27, 30, 32, 33). "I will find my delight in thy command-ments . . . Thy statutes have been my songs" (Verses 47 and 54). "I will never forget thy precepts; for by them thou hast given me life . . . Oh, how I love thy law!" (verses 93 and 97). "I love thy commandments above gold, above fine gold" (verse 127). "His delight is in the law of the Lord" (Psalm 1.2). We cannot fail to see how often the words *love* and *delight* occur. This was no servitude; so far from that it was liberty. "I will keep thy law continually, for ever and ever; and I shall walk at liberty, for I have sought thy precepts" (Psalm 119.44, 45). Obedience to the will of God, as expressed in the Law of God, was for the Jew life's first duty, life's first privilege, life's first delight, and life's only way to true freedom.

It is this very fact which brings us to something which is at the very heart of this petition. The same statement can mean very different things—it can mean almost opposite things—according to the tone of voice in which it is spoken and the feeling in the heart out of which it comes. This petition, "Thy will be done", can mean very different things; the tone of voice in which it is spoken, and the emotion which gave it birth make all the difference.

i. It can be spoken in *bitter resentment*. It can be the statement of one who knows that there is no escape and that there is no other way, but who is filled with rebellious, angry, bitter resentment that it should be so. Life was hard for Beethoven. In particular, it was a terrible fate for one whose very soul was music that he should have to experience complete deafness. It is said that when they found him dead, his fists were clenched, as if he would strike God, and his lips were drawn back in a snarl, as if he would spit his defiance and his bitterness at God. There are many people who know quite well that they must accept the will of God, but who spend their life in bitter resentment that it should be so.

ii. It can be spoken in the tone of one who *resignedly accepts a situation, not so much in bitterness, as because there is nothing else to do but to admit defeat*. Julian was the Roman Emperor who tried to put the clock back. He tried to reverse the decision of Constantine that Christianity should be the religion of the Empire, and he tried to re-introduce the worship and the service and the ceremonies of the ancient gods. In the end he was mortally wounded in battle in the east. The historians tell how, when he lay bleeding to death, he took a handful of his blood and tossed it in the air, saying: "You have conquered, O man of Galilee!" It was not so much that he submitted; it was rather that he wearily accepted defeat, because there was nothing else to do.

Thomas Carlyle could say the bluntest things. He was told of a lavender and lace type of gushing lady who remarked that she accepted the world. "By God," commented Carlyle, "she'd better!"

This is indeed acceptance of the will of God, but it is completely joyless; it is tired and weary and defeated and resigned, not content, still less glad, but only resigned to the fact that things must be so. There are many who live in a grey acceptance that things are as they are.

iii. It can be spoken in the tone of voice of one who *in the end accepts something, not exactly in weary resignation, but in the conviction that he cannot in any event do anything about it,* the tone of voice of one who yields with a more or less good grace to *force majeure.* In *Courage to Change,* her study of Reinhold Neibuhr, June Bingham tells a story which Niebuhr loved to tell. In *Courage to Change,* her study of Reinhold Niebuhr, wanted her to come out for a walk, and she did not want to go. He extolled the virtues of exercise and fresh air, and in the end she came. As they ended their walk, he turned to her and said : " Now aren't you glad that you decided to come?" Whereat his daughter replied : " I didn't decide. You were just bigger !" Her philosophy was that it was better to do without a struggle what in the end you would be compelled to do anyway ! There are some people who accept the will of God just because God is " bigger ". They are not particularly resentful; and they are not particularly defeated and resigned; but equally they have no thrill and throb of joy in making God's will their choice. They could never say : " Oh, how I *love* thy law !"

iv. It can be spoken in a tone of *serene and trustful love and joy and peace.* It can be spoken in the tone of one who is quite sure that " a father's hand will never cause his child a needless tear ". In the days of the Covenanters terrible things happened in Scotland, as the government by the most savage measures tried to crush the Covenanters out of existence. Richard Cameron was one of the most famous and one of the greatest of them. They captured Richard Cameron's son. The son had notably beautiful hands. They cut off the hands and sent them to the father with a kind of wanton cruelty. Richard Cameron recognised them at once. " They are my son's," he said, " my own dear son's. It is the Lord's will and good is the will of the Lord. He has never wronged me or mine." Here is the complete and trusting acceptance of anything that might or could happen, as part of the will of God. As we shall see, there is something more to be said about things like that. But here is neither resentment, nor defeatedness, nor even acceptance; here there is the determination never to doubt the will of God.

Clearly, one question presents itself to be asked— Why is it that we find it so difficult to accept the will of God, and to say: " Thy will be done "? It may well be said that there is one basic sin from which all other sins spring, and that basic sin is the sin of pride. The root reason why we find it so difficult to accept the will of God is that we so often in our heart of hearts think that we know better than God. We really believe that, if we could only get our way, we would be happy, that, if we could only arrange life and the events of life to suit our ideas, everything would be all right. That is why so many people would really rather pray, " Thy will be *changed* " than, " Thy will be *done* ". So long as there is pride and self-will in our hearts we cannot pray this petition, for the simple reason that we do not want to say it, because, whether we admit it or not, we would much prefer our own way, and we think our own way is better. That is one reason for reminding ourselves again and again what God is really like. There are two things in God which, if we really believe them, should make it easy to pray this prayer.

i. We believe in the *wisdom* of God. We believe that

God in his wisdom knows far better than we do what is for our ultimate good. We believe that only God sees all time. In the nature of things we must live in the moment. The past is past and cannot be recalled; we cannot see even a moment ahead. God alone can see the whole pattern of life, and, therefore, God alone can see what is to our ultimate good.

Long before Christianity ever entered this world the Stoics held this point of view. They held, not that God is *Eimarmene*, Fate, but that God is *Pronoia*, Providence. They believed that there was literally absolutely nothing in this world that happened outside the will of God, and that every action and motion of that will was directed towards the good of man. The Stoics could, therefore, say the noblest things. "I have trained myself," said Seneca, "not merely to obey God, but to agree with his decisions. I follow him because my soul wills it, and not because I must" (*Letters* 96.2). "Use me henceforth for whatever thou wilt," prayed Epictetus. "I am thine; I crave exemption from nothing that seems good in thy sight; where thou wilt, lead me; in what thou wilt, clothe me" (*Discourses* 2.16.42). "I have submitted my freedom of choice to God. He wills that I should have fever; it is my will too. He wills that I should get something; it is my will too. He does not will it; I do not wish it" (*Discourses* 4.1.89).

The Stoics went on to argue that, if everything without exception in this world is the result of the will of God, then acceptance is the way to happiness and to freedom. Things *cannot* be changed. Therefore, to accept the will of God is to put yourself in line with the whole universe; to refuse the will of God is to batter your head against the walls of the universe, and, therefore, necessarily to be wretched and unhappy. *Deo parere libertas est,* said Seneca in the famous phrase

(*On the Happy Life* 15.7). To obey God is perfect freedom. In the famous line of the Hymn of Cleanthes, as Seneca quotes it: "*Ducunt volentes fata, nolentem trahunt*" (*Letters* 107.11). Fate leads the willing, but drags the unwilling.

If a heathen can say this, if a man can say this who knows nothing of God in Jesus Christ, how much more should a Christian be able to say it? We may begin by making it our rule to remember always and ever the perfect wisdom of God.

ii. We believe in the *love* of God. Now it is just here that we part company with the Stoics. The Stoic believed that literally everything is in accordance with the will of God, more, that it *is* the will of God. The Stoic then went on to say that a man must teach himself not to care what happened to anyone or to himself or to anything he had, because whatever happened was the will of God. Begin with a broken cup; go on to a torn robe; proceed to the death of a horse or a pet animal; and in the end you will be able to stand and watch your nearest and dearest die, and say, "I don't care, I will not care," for this is the will of God (Epictetus, *Discourses* 1.4.111, 112). Here is something which the Christian cannot and must not say.

Nothing has done the Christian faith and the Church more harm than the indiscriminate and blasphemous use of the phrase, "It is God's will". There are people who will go into a home in which a child has been killed in a street accident, in which a young life has been cut off before it has ever had time to blossom, in which a man or a woman is suffering agonies from some disease that not all the skill of man can help, in which untimely death has reft a mother from her children or a father from the family which was dependent on him, and who will say, "It is God's will". There are those who will hear of a terrible accident on the road, at sea, or in the air, or from some cataclysm in nature and who will say, "It is God's will". Such things are not the will of God. It is not God's will ever that a child should be needlessly killed by some reckless or drunken fool in a motor car, or that some one should be agonised by some disease which is the enemy of life. This is the direct opposite of the will of God; *this is the result of the sin of man,* not necessarily the sin of the sufferer, but the sin of the human situation of which the sufferer is a part. It is precisely such pain and sorrow and suffering that Jesus came to defeat, as his healing and miraculous powers show. It is a blasphemous slander on God to attribute to him acts and situations and events which, if we believe in the love of God in Jesus Christ, are the exact opposite of his will.

It may be the will of God—it often is—that we have to take some heart-breaking decision, that we have to accept some poignant disappointment, that we have to make some agonising sacrifice, that we have to face some way from which our whole being shrinks. It is at such a moment as that, that we must be quite sure of the wise and loving will of God, no matter what it feels like.

But in these moments of human sin and agony and human sorrow, what *do* we say? We have to say: "This is not God's will. This is the result in some way of the sin and the folly of man. You have been bitterly involved in this. God did not send it to you. But God can bring you through it, still erect, still steady-eyed, and still on your own two feet. And more, much more, out of this bitter thing you can come stronger, and purer, and nearer God and better able to help men, than ever you were before. For God can work for good even things that are outside his will, to those who trust and love him." We can say: "If you will allow God to use this and to use you, this, even this, can *become* part of his will."

My mother died of cancer of the spine in such a way and out of such a pain that it was a relief to see her release. She was a saint, and the sorrow was very sore. But I can remember my father coming to me to this day and saying to me: "You will have a new note in your preaching now." And it was so, in the goodness of God, because I was better able to help others who were going through it, because I had gone through it.

iii. So this brings us to the final thing about this petition. When we pray, "Thy will be done", it does not mean that we either wish or expect to be saved from trouble. Here is the lesson of Gethsemane (Matthew 26.34-46). Jesus prayed to be released from his ordeal, but only, if it should be the will of God. He was not released; but he was given the power to go through it. When we pray, "Thy will be done", we are not praying for release; we are not praying for resignation; we are praying for triumph. We are praying not to be taken out of a situation, but to be enabled to face it and conquer it and defeat it.

One of the greatest stories in the Bible is the story of Shadrach, Meshach and Abednego. They were threatened with death in the fiery furnace. Their answer was: "If it be so, our God whom we serve is able to deliver us from the burning fiery furnace; and he will deliver us out of your hand, O king. *But, if not,* be it known to you, O king, we will not serve your gods" (Daniel 3.16-18). *But, if not*—they did not look for escape, they looked for power to face this situation, whatever be the outcome.

The fact of life is quite simple. When the will of God insists that we face some difficult and sore and even agonising situation, there is nothing to stop us running away from it. Jesus could have turned back in Gethsemane. But, if we do run away from it, there can be no happiness in life, for there can be no happiness when a man cannot face either himself or God any longer. But if we do face it, with all it demands, then in life there is a peace and a joy and a satisfaction that nothing else can give. That is why Plato long ago said that the wise man will always prefer to suffer wrong rather than to do wrong, and that is why the whole lesson of the Book of the Revelation is that there is all the difference in the world between *life* and *existence,* and that it may be that, if a man chooses to continue to *exist,* he may well forfeit *life.* To us the choice will not be between life and death, but it may be the choice between comfort and struggle, between ease and sacrifice; and it may well be that if we choose *pleasure,* we shall lose *joy,* for joy is the product of obedience to the will of God.

And how do we attain to this perfect obedience? The Stoics used to say that it was no more than a matter of the will. " Bend your will to it, man," they said, " and you can do it." A man learns to walk by practising walking and to read by practising reading. You can be good by practising goodness, and obedient by practising obedience. We know only too well that there is more to it than that. We know only too well that the human will at best is weak. We can only attain to this submission and loving obedience when we receive Jesus Christ into our hearts, and then he will give us the dynamic to say, as he himself said, " Thy will be done."

GIVE US THIS DAY
OUR DAILY BREAD

It might well be thought that this is the one petition in the Lord's Prayer about the interpretation of which there could be no argument and no dispute. But any such conclusion would be very far from the truth. It would almost be true to say that this petition is the petition about the meaning of which there is most doubt.

i. In the first place, there is doubt as to the actual meaning of it. This doubt becomes quite obvious, if we look at the various translations of it which have been offered by different translators.

It may be said that the translation of the AV, "Give us this day our daily bread", is the standard translation. This is the translation of Tyndale, the Great Bible, the Geneva Bible, the Bishops' Bible of the older translations. It is the translation of the RV, the RSV and of the New English Bible; but the RV notes in the margin an alternative translation, "our bread for the coming day", and the New English Bible gives as an alternative, "our bread for the morrow". On the whole it may be said that all these translations go right back to the Old Latin version of the Bible, which existed long before the Vulgate, and which had in it the phrase *quotidianum panem,* which is literally daily bread.

There is a group of translations all of which are closely connected with this standard translation, and which are variations on it, or slight improvements of it.

Weymouth has : "Give us to-day bread for the day". Moffatt has : "Give us to-day our bread for to-morrow". Goodspeed has : "Give us to-day bread for the day". But there are two other different lines of translation.

The first line is represented by the Twentieth Century New Testament which has "Give us to-day the bread that we shall need", and by E. V. Rieu who has, "Give us the bread of life to-day".

The second line goes back to the Vulgate, and is therefore of very great importance because the Vulgate is the Bible of the Roman Catholic Church. When in the fifth century Jerome produced the Vulgate by a revision of the Old Latin translation he did not keep the phrase *quotidianum panem;* he introduced a much more difficult phrase, *supersubstantialem panem,* super-substantial bread, which must mean bread of more than human, more than physical, more than material, more than earthly substance. This very naturally got into the Roman Catholic translations such as the Rheims. Equally naturally, this was the translation of Wicliffe, because Wicliffe was largely dependent on the Vulgate. He has, "Give us this day our bread over other sub-stance". Ronald Knox in his modern Roman Catholic translation put into the text the standard translation, "Give us this day our daily bread"; but he has a footnote saying that here the word in the Latin is *supersubstantialis,* which, he rightly says, has sometimes been taken as a direct reference to the Holy Eucharist.

Here then is the situation. Upon investigation the simple word *daily* produces a crop of complications. Why should this be so?

The reason for the doubt is this. The Greek word in question is *epiousios*; and the fact is that there is no other occurrence of it in the whole of Greek literature. This is the sole occurrence of the word; it may well have been coined by the man who wrote Matthew's Gospel; and therefore there is no parallel whatsoever which might help us to define its meaning. This statement needs to be slightly—and tantalisingly— qualified. The most valuable aid to the definition of New Testament vocabulary is the help of the papyri, these everyday Greek documents like letters and accounts and legal documents in which we find the Greek of the common people contemporary with the new Testament. In the papyri this word did turn up once in the plural neuter form *ta epiousia,* which seems to mean the requirements for the day. It is actually on a list of things which might be a shopping list. The papyrus has of course been recorded (Preisigke, *Sammelbuch* 5224.20), but the tantalising thing is that the original papyrus has been lost, and it is a tantalising quirk of fortune that the one papyrus which contains this unique Greek word is no longer available for direct examination. But, even so, wherein does the doubt arise, and what is the trouble in defining the meaning of this word? The trouble lies in this. The word *epiousios* is a compound word. The first part of it is the preposition *epi,* which can mean for, towards, upon. The second part of the word is *ousios.* This is a participial form. Now there are two very common Greek verbs *einai,* to be, and *ienai,* to come or to go (the *i* is pronounced separately, *ee—en—ai*). The feminine present participle of *einai* is *ousa,* and the feminine present participle of *ienai* is *iousa.* There is only an *iota* of a difference. The question therefore is whether the preposition *epi* has been combined with the participle of the verb *to be,* and whether therefore *epiousios* has something to do with *being,* or, whether it has been combined with the participle of the verb to come, and whether therefore *epiousios* has something to do with that which is coming.

The interpretations of *epiousios* therefore oscillate between the ideas of *being* and *coming*.

a. If we take it that *epiousios* has to do with *being*, then we will get three main ideas.

First, the prayer may mean bread for our physical being, bread to keep us in being, to keep us alive, bread for our day to day needs.

Second, the prayer may mean bread for our essential being, for our spiritual being. This then will be a prayer for the " supersubstantial " bread, the bread that is real, essential, spiritual bread for our spiritual nourishment and growth.

Third, it is just barely possible that we might take *epi* in the sense of *near,* a sense which it can have. It would then be a prayer for the bread which is near, the bread that lies to hand; and that presumably would be a prayer for the simple needs of life, for the things which are obtainable by all, as opposed to recondite luxuries. It would then be a prayer for the simple, basic needs of life.

b. If we take it that *epiousios* has the sense of coming, then the prayer will be for bread for the coming day. This meaning is made the more likely in that *he epiousa* is the Greek for the morrow, the coming day. *Hemera* is the Greek for day and the full phrase would be *he epiousa hemera,* but the *hemera* is regularly left to be understood.

We must now come to a decision. Which of the two lines is more likely?

It is not really doubtful that it is the second of the two lines which is the more likely. The two possibilities are that the word *epiousios* is a compound of *epi* + *ousa* or of *epi* + *iousa*. Now by the laws of Greek word formation if *epi* were combined with *ousa,* the *i* of the *epi* would be elided and the resultant word would be *epousa*; whereas if *epi* were combined with *iousa*, there being two *i*'s, one of them would remain. The conclusion then is that *epiousios* has to do with *coming*, and that therefore the phrase means *bread for the coming day*. If then the prayer is prayed in the morning, it will be a prayer for the needs of the day; if it is prayed in the evening, it will be a prayer for the needs of to-morrow.

ii. We turn now to the meaning of the petition.

(a) It has been taken as a prayer for " the Sacrament of Christ's Body which we receive daily " (Augustine, *The Sermon on the Mount* 2.7.25). Augustine tells us that in his time (the fifth century) the Communion was received in some places daily, in some places at certain intervals (*Sermons on John* 26.15; Letter 54, *To Ianuarius* 2). His own attitude was that it should be received daily. In an Easter Sermon (*Sermon* 227) to the newly baptised members of his congregation he said : " You should realise what you have received, what you will receive in the future, what you ought to receive daily."

So, if that meaning be taken, then this is a prayer for the bread of the Sacrament taken in daily communion with Christ and with his people. It is to be noted that Augustine well knew that daily Communion was not the universal custom of the Church, and he did not claim that this was the only meaning of the petition, for if it were the only meaning then there would be large numbers of Christians who would be unable to pray it.

(b) It has been taken as a prayer for spiritual food, and in particular for the spiritual food of the word of God in Scripture. As Augustine says, it is a prayer for " spiritual food, namely, the divine precepts which we are to think over and to put into practice each day " (*The Sermon on the Mount* 2.7.27). This would be as the hymn has it :

> *Break thou the bread of life,*
>   *Dear Lord, to me,*
> *As thou didst break the loaves*
>   *Beside the sea;*
> *Beyond the sacred page*
>   *I seek thee, Lord,*
> *My spirit pants for thee,*
>   *O living word.*

On this interpretation the idea would be that the spiritual life of man is starved and stunted, unless it is daily nourished by the word of God in Scripture in the Bible; it is a prayer that our minds and hearts should be daily enriched in growth by the study of the word of God and the meditation upon it.

(c) This very naturally brings us to the interpretation that this is a prayer for nothing less than and nothing other than Christ himself. " I am the Bread of Life," Jesus said. " He who comes to me shall never hunger, and he who believes in me shall never thirst " (John 6.35). Our daily bread is nothing less than Christ, the Bread of life. On this interpretation we would have the same picture as is in Matthew Arnold's poem *East London*:

> *'Twas August, and the fierce sun overhead*
> *Smote on the squalid streets of Bethnal Green,*
> *And the pale weaver, through his windows seen*
> *In Spitalfields, look'd thrice dispirited.*
> *I met a preacher there I knew, and said:*
> *" Ill and o'er-worked, how fare you in this scene?"*
> *" Bravely!" said he; " for I of late have been*
> *Much cheer'd by thoughts of Christ, the living*
>   *bread."*

And indeed it is truest of all that we cannot live without the strength and help which we can daily draw from Jesus Christ.

(d) We need not for a moment deny that all these

meanings may be in this petition. But we believe that the meaning of this petition is much simpler than any of these things. We believe that it is just what it says, that it is a petition for daily bread, a petition that God should give to us the simple, ordinary things which we daily need to keep body and soul together. It is in fact one of the most precious things in life that we can take the simple, ordinary things to God, that God is not only the God of the great world-shaking, epoch-making events, but that he is also the God who cares that his humblest child may have daily bread to eat. If we take this petition in that simple sense, certain things emerge from it.

1. We must note right at the beginning that we are taught to pray, not, Give *me my* daily bread, but, Give *us our* daily bread. "A man" runs the Jewish saying, "should always join himself with the community in his prayers." The very use of the plural precludes all selfishness in prayer. One of the most tragic features of present day society is what one can only call an essential mutual disregard. It is characteristic of our age that one class of the community does not care what happens to another class so long as its needs are met, one trade in the community does not care what happens to other trades so long as its demands are met. Life is pervaded with essential selfishness.

But he who prays this petition by the very form of the words is committed to a life in which he cannot have too much while others have too little, a life in which a war on want and the determination to bring bread to the hungry become for him inescapable duties. The man who in praying this petition thinks only of his bread has no real conception of what the petition means.

2. The prayer is for our *daily* bread. It does not look fearfully into the distant future; it is content to take the present and to leave it in the hands of God. "Don't

worry about to-morrow," Jesus said (Matthew 6.34).
Take it a day at a time. Gregory of Nyssa in commenting on this passage says (*The Lord's Prayer, Sermon* 4) :
" God says to you as it were : He who gives you the day
will give you also the things necessary for the day."
" Who causes the sun to rise?" he goes on. " Who makes
the darkness of the night to disappear? Who shows
you the rays of light? Who revolves the sky so that
the source of light is above the earth? Does he who
gives you so great things need your help to supply for
the needs of your body?" This is a petition which no
man can pray, unless he is prepared to live a day at a
time. As Newman had it in his hymn :

I do not ask to see
The distant scene,—one step enough for me.

Marcus Aurelius laid it down that all that any man
possesses is the instant of time in which at the very
moment he is; the past is past and cannot be recalled;
the future is necessarily unknown; and in this prayer
a man takes his moment, which is all he has, and rests
it in the goodness and the mercy and the bounty of
God.

3. Gregory of Nyssa in the sermon which we have
already quoted stresses the fact that the prayer is for
bread. The truly Christian man does not pray for
luxuries; what he prays for is the simple food which
is enough for life. " So we say to God : Give us
bread. Not delicacies or riches, nor magnificent purple
robes, golden ornaments or precious stones or silver
dishes. Nor do we ask him for landed estates, or military
commands, or political leadership. We pray neither for
herds of horses and oxen or other cattle in great numbers, nor for a host of slaves. We do not say, give us
a prominent position in assemblies or monuments and
statues raised to us, nor silken robes and musicians at
meals, nor any other thing by which the soul is estranged

from the thought of God and higher things; no—but only bread!" We do not pray for luxuries in order that "the stomach, this perpetual tax collector, may live daintily through all this." He gives the advice: "Cling only to what is necessary." Immediately we go beyond that, desire and covetousness creep into life, and life is distracted and distressed. Immediately we want more than our neighbour and set our own luxury in the fore-front life goes wrong. "So someone must weep, his neighbour must sorrow, many who are deprived of their property must be miserable, in order that their tears may contribute to enhance the ostentatious display of his table." It is the simple things, the things for which nature itself supplies the flavouring, for which we are to ask, and with which we must be content. The prayer is for the satisfaction of simple need, not for the service of selfish luxury.

4. There can be few passages in the Bible which better illustrate the meaning of the word *Give* than this passage does. Jesus taught us to pray, Give us this day our daily bread; but, if we prayed this petition and then simply sat down with folded hands and waited, we would quite certainly starve. The food is not going to appear all ready-made on our tables; God is not going to spoon feed any man; prayer is never the easy way to get God to do for us what we can well do, and must certainly do for ourselves. What this prayer does teach is that apart from and without God there would be no such things as food at all. It is God alone who has the secret of life, and God alone has the gift of making living things. No man ever made a living and a grow-ing thing. In the most literal sense all food comes from God. The scientist can construct a synthetic seed which will have exactly the same chemical analysis as a real seed; but there will be one all-important difference— the synthetic seed will not grow. This petition acknow-

ledges in full man's dependence on God and man's debt to God.

But there is the other side of the matter. If we would have our food, we must work for it. If God's seed is to grow, man must till the ground and prepare the soil and care for it and tend it. God's giving and man's toiling must go hand in hand; and the more man toils, the more God opens his hand and pours out his gifts upon him.

To pray, Give us this day our daily bread, is at one and the same time to express our dependence on God, our trust in God, and to challenge ourselves to the effort and the toil which will bring the gifts of God to ourselves, and through us to our fellowmen.

Give us this day our daily bread—in praying this petition we in trust ask God to supply all the physical and the spiritual needs of this life, we commit ourselves to the service of our fellowmen, and we pledge ourselves to the effort of mind and of body which will make it possible for God to give us more and more that our own lives may be enriched and that through us God's gifts may be shared with others.

FORGIVEN AND FORGIVING

Forgive us our debts, as we forgive our debtors (Matthew 6.12 AV). It has been well pointed out that the position of this petition in the Lord's Prayer is peculiarly appropriate. As Plummer points out, *forgiving* follows immediately on the heels of *giving*. The previous petition asked God *to give* us our daily bread; this petition asks him *to forgive* us for our sins. Tertullian says: " It is fitting that after contemplating the liberality of God we should likewise address his clemency " (*On Prayer* 7). It is the more fitting in that when we remember the richness and the bounty of God's mercy we are all the more shamed by the memory of how little we deserve it.

This is the only petition of the Lord's Prayer which has two distinct and equally used forms, and this is true of each half of it. At the moment we look only at the first half. Sometimes the first half is prayed in the form of the AV : " Forgive us our *debts,* as we forgive our *debtors.*" Sometimes it is prayed in the form which in ancient translations appears only in Tyndale and in modern translations occurs only in Knox : " Forgive us our *trespasses,* as we forgive them that *trespass* against us." If we add to these two forms the form of the petition given in Luke's version of the prayer, we get still a third form : " Forgive us our *sins;* for we also forgive everyone that is *indebted* to us " (Luke 11.4). And in this petition the New English Bible moves furthest from the traditional renderings : " Forgive us *the wrong that we have done,* as we have forgiven

those who have wronged us." It will be well to begin
by trying to define the meaning, and by trying to see
the reasons for the divergent translations.

In the body of the prayer in Matthew 6.12 the
word in question is *opheilemata* which is the plural
of *opheilema*. *Opheilema* is a word with a wide range
of meanings all grouped round one common and un-
changing idea. It always denotes something which is
owed, something which is due, something which it is
a duty or an obligation to give or to pay. In other
words, it means a debt in the widest sense of the term.
At its narrowest it is a money debt; at its widest it is
any moral or religious obligation which a man in
duty must discharge.

Opheilema is rare in biblical language. In the New
Testament it occurs only once (Romans 4.4), and in
the Old Testament it occurs only once (Deuteronomy
24.10), and in both places it has the sense of a money
debt. The corresponding verb is *opheilein,* which means
to owe, and which can be used in all the senses of the
English word *ought*. It occurs more than 30 times
in the New Testament, 8 times in the sense of owing
money, and 25 times in the sense of moral or religious
obligation.

We may look at certain examples of *opheilema* in
secular Greek to see the width of its meaning. In
the papyri it is often used in business documents of
financial debts. Thucydides uses it of the duty of repay-
ing kindness received (2.40). Plato uses it of a child's
obligation to pay the debt he owes to his parents (*Laws*
717B). Aristotle uses it of the kind of financial debt
which in all normal circumstances must be repaid
(*Nicomachean Ethics* 1165a 3). *Opheilema* is that which
is owed, that which a man ought to give or to pay, that
which it is a moral or religious duty to give. Forgive
us, says this petition, for every failure in duty, for

failure to render to God and to man that which we ought to have rendered, for the debt to God and to man which we owe and which we have failed to pay.

We now turn to Luke's version (11.4). Luke has it: "Forgive us our sins." The word that Luke uses is *hamartia*, which is the commonest of all Greek words for sin. *Hamartia* was not originally an ethical word; originally it meant quite simply *a missing of the mark*, as when a javelin, or an arrow, or a blow misses its mark. In this sense, sin is a failure to hit the mark, a failure to realise the true aim of life, a failure to be and to do that which we ought to have done, and which we could have been and could have done. It can seem that, though they are based on different pictures, *opheilema* and *hamartia* are not radically different in meaning.

It so happens that it is quite possible to explain why Matthew used the one and Luke the other. Jesus, of course, did not give the Lord's Prayer to his disciples in Greek; he gave it in Aramaic. Now in the time of Jesus in Palestine the Rabbis thought of sin almost exclusively as a failure in obedience to God. To them goodness was obedience, sin was disobedience. This is to say that man's first obligation is to give God obedience; not to give obedience to God is to be in debt to God; and therefore their commonest word for sins was *choba'*, which in fact means *debt*. This is to say, that it would be quite correct to translate Matthew's *opheilemata* by the word *sins*, because it is exactly the Greek equivalent of the Aramaic *choba'*, which is literally a *debt*, but which is the commonest rabbinic word for *sin*. There is then no difference at all between Matthew and Luke; they are simply both translating the Aramaic *choba'*, and Matthew, being characteristically Jewish, chooses a Greek word meaning *debts*, while

Luke, being characteristically Greek, uses a more general Greek word for sin.

This explains Matthew and Luke, and it also completely justifies the NEB rendering, but it still leaves the rendering *trespasses* unexplained. The truth is that linguistically speaking there is no justification whatever for the use of the word *trespasses* to render the Greek word *opheilemata*. How then did *trespasses* get into the text? As we have seen, its first appearance in the English Bible is with Tyndale, and of the translators ancient and modern only Ronald Knox retained it. It may be that Tyndale inserted *trespasses* into the text of the prayer on the strength of the amplification in Matthew 6.14, 15 : "For if ye forgive men their *trespasses*, your heavenly Father will also forgive you : but if ye forgive not men their *trespasses*, neither will your Father forgive your *trespasses*." There the word in Greek is *paraptomata*, which means properly a false step, a slip, a blunder. It can, for instance, be used for a slip in grammar (Longinus, *On the Sublime* 36.2), and it could quite reasonably be translated *trespasses*. Although the words are different, it may be that Tyndale took the word into the prayer from the amplification. Why should he do so? It may well be that Tyndale did not wish to use the word *debts*, because there were those who desired to take this petition, " Forgive us our debts, as we forgive our debtors ", as a statement that debts in the money sense of the term are obliterated and need no longer be paid. Augustine (*The Sermon on the Mount* 2.8) in point of fact spends the greater part of his exposition of this petition dealing with the obviously not inconvenient interpretation which found in this petition a new way to abolish old debts.

From the purely linguistic point of view, in the text of the Lord's Prayer in this petition *debts* is a correct rendering, *trespasses* is not justifiable, and it may well be that *sins* would give the meaning most simply, most unmistakably, and not inaccurately.

We must now turn directly to the meaning and the interpretation.

i. " Pray then like this," said Jesus; and one of the things which we are to pray is, " Forgive us our debts." Jesus bade all men to pray that prayer without distinction. He did not say that this is the prayer which sinners ought to pray; he said that this is the prayer that all men ought to pray.

That is the proof of the universality of sin. Luther commenting on this petition said : " We must note how here again the indigence of our miserable life is indicated; we are in the land of debts, we are up to the ears in sin." To ask forgiveness for sin is in itself a confession of sin. Tertullian said : " A petition for pardon is itself a full confession, because he who begs for pardon fully admits his guilt " (*On Prayer* 7).

The Bible is never afraid to show its great men under the consciousness of sin. " Depart from me," Peter cried out to Jesus, " for I am a sinful man " (Luke 5.8). " Christ Jesus came into the world to save sinners," said Paul. " And I am the foremost of sinners " (1 Timothy 1.15). " If we say we have no sin," writes John, " we deceive ourselves, and the truth is not in us. If we confess our sin, he is faithful and just, and will forgive us our sins and cleanse us from all unrighteousness " (1 John 1.8, 9). The people who are condemned are people like the Pharisee who contentedly thanked God that he was not as other men are, and certainly not like the tax-gatherer weeping for his sins (Luke 18.9-14). It is the young man who blandly claimed that he had kept all the commandments who went away sorrowful (Matthew 19.16-22; Mark 10.17-22; Luke 18.18-23).

The fact that Jesus taught all men to pray this

prayer shows the universality of sin; and to pray this prayer a sense of sin is a prior requirement. This therefore is an impossible prayer for a generation which, in the famous phrase of Sir Oliver Lodge, is not worrying about its sins. Since then there can be no asking for forgiveness without the consciousness of sin, it may well be said that to be conscious of no sin is the greatest sin of all.

Origen (*On Prayer* 28.1-5), in order to awaken the sense of sin, enumerates the debts which every man owes simply because he is a man. He uses the famous threefold classification. *A man owes a debt to his fellowman.* He owes a debt to his fellow-christians, to his fellow-citizens, and to all men. He owes a debt to strangers, to the aged, to those of his own family such as his sons and his brothers. There is in life a whole series of "obligations, contracted through the spirit of wisdom, and bound to issue in charity." *A man owes a debt to himself.* He owes a debt to his body, not to waste its strength and health in injuring pleasure. He owes a debt to his mind, to use it in such a way that it retains its keenness. He owes a debt to his soul, for he must tend his soul carefully. *A man owes a debt to God.* Because God made us in his image we must love him with heart and soul and mind and strength (Mark 12.30; Luke 10.27; Matthew 22.37). He owes a debt to Jesus Christ who purchased us at the price of his own blood (Acts 20.28; 1 Peter 1.18, 19; Revelation 5.9). He owes a debt to the Holy Spirit whom he must not grieve (Ephesians 4.30). Origen has the odd but lovely idea that a man owes a debt to the angel who looks after him and protects him (Matthew 18.10). Origen quotes 1 Corinthians 4.9, which says that we have become a spectacle to the world, to angels and to men. We are, he says, like actors in some great and crowded theatre who owe a debt to the spectators to act out the play as well as possible. Even so, we must play out the drama of life nobly for the sake of those who in heaven and upon earth look on. Apart from these general debts, we have debts to the widow and orphan, to the deacon, the priest and the bishop, and husband and wife owe a debt to each other (1 Corinthians 7.3, 5). "While a man is alive," says Origen, "there is not a single hour, day or night, when he is not a debtor." The very fact that we are set in the human situation has put us under a series of debts which no man can ever fully repay. A man in the nature of things is bound to be a defaulter, and therefore in the nature of things is bound to stand in need of forgiveness.

Gregory of Nyssa (*Sermons on the Lord's Prayer* 5) presses home on man his debt. Man owes a debt to God, because man has separated himself from his Maker, and deserted to the enemy, and has thus become a runaway and an apostate from his natural Master. Man has exchanged the liberty of free-will for the wicked slavery of sin and has preferred the tyranny of the power of destruction to the companionship of God. The very fact that man has gone his own way puts him in debt to God.

The very constitution of man makes him a sinner. Gregory of Nyssa has a curious interpretation of Jeremiah 9.21, which says that "death is come in through the window." The windows are the senses; it is through the senses that sin and therefore death gain an entry into life. Man in his very being is necessarily open to the invasion of sin.

Any man who honestly faces the human situation cannot be other than conscious of his debt, and of his need to pray to be forgiven.

ii. When we examine the second part of this petition we find that there are two forms of it. The two forms are exemplified by the renderings of the AV and the RSV. The AV renders:

Forgive us our debts as *we forgive* our debtors.
The RSV renders:

Forgive us our debts as *we also have forgiven* our debtors.

In the first instance the verb is in the present tense; in the second it is in the past tense. We find the translations divided between these two forms. The present tense is the translation of all the older versions, Wilcliffe, Tyndale, the Rheims, the Geneva, the Great Bible, the Bishops' Bible; of the modern translations Kingsley Williams and Ronald Knox retain the present. The majority of the modern translations have the past tense, E. V. Rieu, Weymouth, Moffatt, Goodspeed. The NEB renders:

Forgive us the wrong we have done,

As we have forgiven those who have wronged us.

The difference here is not due to a difference in the mind of the various translators; it is due to a variant reading in the Greek text. Certain manuscripts read the present tense (*aphiomen*), we forgive, and certain manuscripts read the perfect tense *aphekamen*, we have forgiven. On the whole, the better manuscripts read the past tense, and the more correct reading is, " as we have forgiven."

In point of actual meaning the variation makes no great difference. In the one case we ask God to forgive us as it is our practice to forgive other people; in the other we ask God to forgive us as we have in fact forgiven others before we make our own prayer.

There is a further question as to how we are to interpret the " as ". Does the " as " express *similarity* or *proportion*? Does the petition mean: " Forgive us in the same way as we have forgiven others?" Or, does it mean: " Forgive us in proportion as we have forgiven others?" There are two things which will help us to come to a decision. In Luke's version (Luke 11.4) there is no ambiguity. Luke's version reads with unimportant variations in all translations: "Forgive us our sins; *for* we also forgive everyone that is indebted to us." Or, as the NEB has it: "Forgive us our sins for we too forgive all who have done us wrong." In the Luke version we acknowledge that we have no right at all to pray for forgiveness for our own sins before we have forgiven those who have done us wrong. In it we come to God telling him that we have forgiven before we even ask for his forgiveness. The second thing which helps us is the expansion and amplification of this petition which follows the prayer: "For if ye forgive men their trespasses, your heavenly Father will also forgive you; but if ye forgive not men their trespasses, neither will your Father forgive your trespasses" (Matthew 6.14, 15). Or, as the NEB has it: "For if you forgive others the wrongs they have done, your heavenly Father will also forgive you; but if you do not forgive others, the wrongs you have done will not be forgiven by your Father" (Matthew 6.14, 15).

The variations in reading and the variations in meaning do not effectively alter the basic significance of the petition. No matter what the reading, and no matter what the precise meaning of the "as", the basic fact is that there is the closest possible connection between human and divine forgiveness, and that he who is unforgiving has cut himself off from the forgiveness of God. However we take this petition we cannot evade the truth that to be forgiven we must be forgiving. And this presents us with a truth so challenging and even so threatening that we are not surprised to find that Chrysostom tells us that in his day there were many who suppressed this clause of the Lord's Prayer altogether.

The connection between human and divine forgiveness is deeply ingrained into New Testament thought. The parable of the unforgiving debtor clearly lays it down that an unforgiving man can hope for no forgiveness (Matthew 18.23-35). As a man judges others, so he will be judged himself, and in matters of mercy he will get what he gives (Matthew 7.1, 2; Mark 4.24; Luke 6.37.38). It is the merciful who will receive mercy (Matthew 5.7). "Judgment is without mercy to one who has shown no mercy" (James 2.13).

This was in fact a legacy of Jewish thought. The rabbinic teaching is full of the conviction that the merciful man will receive the mercy of God, and that the merciless man has cut himself off from the mercy of God. Gamaliel said : "So long as you are merciful, God will have mercy upon you, and if you are not merciful, he will not be merciful to you." Raba said: "Whom does God forgive? Him who overlooks the transgressions of others." "So long as a man remains in his stiffness God does not forgive him." "Whenever you have pity God forgives you." "Learn to receive suffering, and to forgive those who insult you." "Even if a man pays compensation to another whom he has injured, he is not forgiven by God, till he seeks forgiveness from the man he has insulted." And it is interesting to note that this saying goes on to lay it down, that if the injured party, when asked to do so, refuses to forgive, *he* is to be regarded as merciless. Rabbi Zutra's goodnight prayer before sleeping was : "Forgiven is everyone who has done me an injury." The Day of Atonement was the day on which the grand act of atonement for sins known and unknown, sins realised and sins unrealised, the total sin of the community was carried out in the Temple, and which continues to be observed by almost every Jew is this day. Yet it is laid down that the Day of Atonement is unavail-

ing unless a man has appeased and sought the pardon
of the neighbour whom he has wronged. Later Gregory
of Nyssa was to say that a man's prayer for forgiveness cannot be heard when the voice of him whom he
has wronged is drowning it (*Sermons on the Lord's
Prayer* 5). Maybe the noblest statement of this is in
The Wisdom of the Ben Sirach :

He that takes vengeance will suffer from the Lord,
    and he will firmly establish his sins.
Forgive your neighbour the wrong he has done,
    and then your sins will be pardoned when you
        pray.
Does a man harbour anger against another,
    and yet seek for healing from the Lord?
Does he have no mercy toward a man like himself,
    and yet pray for his own sins?
If he himself, being flesh, maintains wrath,
    who will make expiation for his sins?
                            (Ecclesiasticus 28.1-5).

Divine and human forgiveness are one and indivisible.

There is then no evading the principle that the
condition of forgiveness is the forgiving spirit. Long ago
Gregory of Nyssa (*Sermons on the Lord's Prayer* 5)
pointed out that it could not be otherwise for the very
simple and the very fundamental reason that there can
be no fellowship between opposites. " It is impossible
that a wicked man should be intimate with a good man,
or that some one wallowing in impure thoughts should
be friends with some one who is perfectly pure. Thus
a callous man trying to approach God is far from
the divine charity . . . Therefore it is absolutely
necessary that a man who approaches the charity of
God should rid himself of callousness." It is impossible
that a merciless man should have fellowship with the
divine mercy, or a loveless man fellowship with the
divine love, or an unforgiving man with the God whose

name is Saviour and who delights to forgive. The very nature of God is such that between him and the unforgiving man there is a self-erected barrier.

iii. It thus becomes clear that there is in this petition a certain danger. " Forgive us our debts, as we forgive our debtors." The petition asks God to forgive us as we forgive others. This can only mean that if we are unforgiving, if we pray this when we are in a state of bitterness towards a fellowman, we are deliberately asking God *not* to forgive us.

Luther connects this petition with the saying in the Psalms which says of the wicked man : " Let his prayer be counted as sin !" (Psalms 109.7). When this prayer is prayed by a bitter and an unforgiving man it becomes a sin. " Psalm 109.7 says his prayer will be a sin in the sight of God; for what else canst thou mean when thou sayest, ' I will not forgive ', and yet standest before God with thy Pater Noster, and babblest, ' Forgive us our debts, as we forgive our debtors ', than, ' O God, I am thy debtor, and I also have a debtor; I am not willing to forgive him, therefore do thou also not forgive me : I will not obey thee though thou shouldst declare me pardoned; I would rather renounce thine heaven and everything else, and go to the devil ' ?" It is a dreadful thought that a man should ask God *not* to forgive him, and yet that is precisely what the unforgiving man does when he prays this prayer.

In the South Sea Islands in Tahiti it was Robert Louis Stevenson's custom to have family worship each day and in it to have the Lord's Prayer. One day in the middle of the prayer he rose from his knees and left the room. His wife hurried after him thinking that he was ill. " What is the matter?" she said. " Are you ill?" " No," he answered, " but I am not fit to pray the Lord's Prayer to-day." How often that must be true of all of us! Of all prayers the Lord's Prayer can least be used unthinkingly. Once General Oglethorpe remarked to John Wesley: "I never forgive", whereat Wesley answered: "Then I hope, sir, you never sin."

A man has to examine himself before he dares to pray this prayer, for in this petition a man becomes nothing less than his own judge. As Chrysostom had it: "God makes you arbiter of the judgment; as you judge yourself, so he will judge you." Gregory of Nyssa (*Sermons on the Lord's Prayer* 5) writes: "Be yourself your own judge; give yourself the sentence of acquittal. Do you want your debts to be forgiven by God? Forgive them yourself and God will ratify it. For your judgment of your neighbour, which is in your own power, whatever it may be, will call forth the coresponding judgment upon you. What you decide for yourself will be confirmed by the divine judgment." This is only another instance of the universal rule that God's attitude to any man is determined by that man's attitude to his fellowmen. There is a very real sense in which we are every day engaged in judging ourselves.

iv. There is one last comment on this clause of the Lord's Prayer which is the boldest and the most startling of all. It is again in the sermon of Gregory of Nyssa which we have already quoted. Gregory writes: "Jesus wants your disposition to be a good example to God! We invite God to imitate us—'Do thou the same as I have done. Imitate thy servant, O Lord, though he be only a poor beggar, and thou art the King of the Universe. I have shown great mercy to my neighbour—imitate thy servant's charity, O Lord!'" It is in fact the tremendous and audacious leap of this petition that it does ask God to treat us as we have treated others. We may hesitate to put the matter in so starkly startling a way as Gregory put it; but one fact remains. Forgiveness is the very prerogative of God. "Who can forgive sins but God alone?" asked the Jews. In this prayer there is laid upon us the duty of forgiving the sins of others. And this fact is for ever true, that a man is never closer and more kin to God than when he forgives a fellowman.

Forgive us our debts as we forgive our debtors—herein we confess our own sin, and herein we accept the fact that only the forgiving can be forgiven. Herein we follow the example of God. As Paul had it: "Be kind to one another, tenderhearted, forgiving one another, as God in Christ forgave you" (Ephesians 4.32). A Jewish Rabbi once said: "He who hears himself cursed, and has the opportunity to stop the man who curses him, and yet keeps silence, makes himself a partner with God." We are the disciples of him who prayed for forgiveness for those who were nailing him to a cross (Luke 23.34). If we would imitate our Lord, and if we would be kin to God, we must forgive, and he who forgives will find for himself the forgiveness of God.

THE ORDEAL OF TEMPTATION

Lead us not into temptation, but deliver us from evil (Matthew 6.13 AV). We may begin by noting that there are certain variations in the translation of this petition of the Lord's Prayer.

The petition falls into two clauses. First, Lead us not into temptation. This translation goes very far back and lasts right down into the modern translations. It is the translation of Wicliffe, Tyndale, the Great Bible, the Bishops' Bible. It is the translation of the Rheims and the Geneva Bibles with the unimportant variation of *tentation* for *temptation*. It is the translation of Moffatt and Knox and of Kingsley Williams. The variations on this translation are in the word *Lead* and the word *temptation*. The Revised Version has: "*Bring* us not into temptation". Rieu, Weymouth and the New English Bible all have the word bring instead of lead. Ferrar Fenton has: "Let us not be led into temptation." E. J. Goodspeed has: "Do not subject us to temptation." C. C. Torrey, basing his translation on a hypothetical Aramaic original, has: "Let us not yield to temptation." Two modern translations alter the word *temptation*. E. V. Rieu has: "Do not bring us to *ordeal*." And the New English Bible has: "Do not bring us to the *test*."

The second clause is, "But deliver us from evil." In this clause the renderings vary between *evil*, as a perfectly general term including all evil, and *the Evil One*, meaning Satan or the Devil, the personal power of evil. There is a real doubt here, and some of the translations which insert one of the two translations in the text have the other in the margin. *Evil,* as a general term, is the translation of Wicliffe, Tyndale, the Rheims, the Geneva, the Great Bible, the Bishops' Bible, the RSV (margin, the evil one), E. V. Rieu, Ferrar Fenton (that evil), Moffatt and Knox. *The Evil One,* in the sense of Satan, the Devil, is the translation of The Revised Version, Weymouth (margin, evil), Kingsley Williams, E. J. Goodspeed, and the New English Bible.

As we shall come to see, some of these variations are not unimportant in the task of tracking down the real significance of this petition.

It would be true to say that this is the most natural and instinctive petition in the Lord's Prayer. It is, says Chrysostom, the natural appeal of human weakness and human danger. And yet the odd fact is that this petition has involved more argument and more explanation than any other petition. It is perfectly true that when instinct gives place to reason this petition does involve us in puzzling questions. The difficulties are twofold.

i. How can we reasonably pray not to be lead into temptation when in point of fact temptation is so integral to human existence on earth that we cannot conceive of life without it? As Origen pointed out (*On Prayer* 29.5) the Septuagint (Greek) version of Job 7.1 can be translated: " Is not man's life on earth one continuous temptation?" Origen goes on : " Has anyone ever thought man to be beyond temptations of which he was aware from the day he attained to reason? Is there any time when a man is sure that he has not to struggle against sinning?" It is quite simply impossible to think of human existence without temptation.

Further, and, as we shall come to see this is of the first importance, in Greek the word *trial* and the word *temptation* are the same word (*peirasmos*); and again and again the Bible points out the supreme value of trial. "When he has tried me," said Job, "I shall come forth as gold" (Job 23.10). "Count it all joy, my brethren," said James, "when you meet various trials, for you know that the testing of your faith produces steadfastness" (James 1.2). "In this," writes Peter, "you rejoice, though now for a little while you may have to suffer various trials, so that the genuineness of your faith, more precious than gold which though perishable is tested by fire, may redound to praise and glory and honour at the revelation of Jesus Christ" (1 Peter 1.6, 7). In all these cases the word for trial is *peirasmos*, which is the very same word as is used for *temptation* in this clause of the Lord's Prayer.

The undoubted teaching of life is that life is inconceivable without temptation, and the undoubted teaching of Scripture is that, if temptation were removed from life something irreplaceable would be lost with it.

ii. When we come to think of it, this is on the face of it an extraordinary prayer to pray, for in what sense can we ever believe that God would lead us into temptation? How could God ever be responsible for the attempt to seduce man into sin? As Tertullian (*On Prayer* 8) said: "Far be the thought that the Lord should seem to tempt anyone, as if he were ignorant of the faith of any, or else were eager to overthrow it." This is indeed a difficulty so acute that we are driven to examine more closely the meaning of the words of this petition in order to see if there is a meaning in it which our English versions find it difficult to express. Let us then examine the word which is rendered *temptation*.

The word which is rendered temptation is *peirasmos*. *Peirasmos* is a noun, and like all Greek nouns which end in *-asmos* it describes a process. It is common in biblical literature, but it is not common in secular literature, and we will get the basic idea which lies behind it and which lies behind this petition better, if we examine the verb with which it is connected. The verb is *peirazein*. It may be said that the Greek verb *peirazein* has all the many senses of the English verb *to try*.

(a) It can mean quite simply *to try* or *to attempt* to do something. So it is used in the sentence: "They *attempted* to go into Bithynia" (Acts 16.7). This use is not specially relevant for our investigation.

(b) It regularly means *to test* or *to prove*. In this sense it can be used as exactly parallel to the verb *dokimazein*, which is the word for testing or proving the quality of a metal, the genuineness or otherwise of a coin. In this sense *peirazein* can be used, for instance, for the process of testing the effects of a drug by experiment in its use. It is said that when the Queen of Sheba heard of the wisdom of Solomon she came "*to test* him with hard questions" (1 Kings 10.1; cp. 2 Chronicles 9.1). It is said that the Church at Ephesus has *tested* those who claim to be apostles, and who are not, and has found them false (Revelation 2.2). 2 Corinthians 13.5 is a very good example of this: "Examine (*peirazein*) yourselves, to see whether you are holding to your faith. *Test* yourselves (*dokimazein*)." *Peirazein* describes the process by which the genuineness of anything or anyone is tested, and thereby proved or disproved.

(c) In the Bible *peirazein* is often used of God's testing of men to see whether or not their faith is genuine, loyal, and true. It is forbidden to listen to a false prophet or to a dreamer of dreams. When such a man emerges, "The Lord your God is *testing* you to know whether you love the Lord your God with all your heart and with all your soul" (Deuteronomy 13.3). So God *tested* Abraham by seeming to demand the sacrifice of Isaac

(Genesis 22.1). God does not allow us to be *tested* beyond that which we can bear (1 Corinthians 10.13).

This meaning is very important; it is the more important because in the AV *test* and *tempt* are used in the same sense, as they were in Elizabethan English. For instance, in Genesis 22.1 which we have already quoted the AV has, "God did *tempt* Abraham". It is clearly impossible to think of God trying to seduce Abraham into sinning; the meaning here is *test*. In point of fact, on at least twenty occasions the RSV alters an AV *tempt* into *test*.

Peirazein is regularly used of the divine placing of a man in a situation which is a test, a situation in which he *may* fall, but in which he is not *meant* to fall, a situation which *may* be his ruin, but out of which he is *meant* to emerge spiritually strengthened and enriched. It is used of a situation into which temptation to disloyalty certainly enters, but the characteristic of which is not so much temptation as it is testing.

(d) *Peirazein* is frequently used in the New Testament of the action of men who maliciously cross-examine or otherwise test some one with the deliberate intention of catching him out or making him incriminate himself. In this sense it is repeatedly used of the Scribes and Pharisees asking Jesus questions which were designed to entrap him (Matthew 16.1; 19.3; 12.18).

(e) *Peirazein* is frequently used of the direct and deliberate seduction to sin which in English is the normal meaning of the word to tempt. Husbands and wives are not to deny each other their natural rights except by agreement, "lest Satan tempt you through lack of self-control" (1 Corinthians 7.5). In this sense Satan is pre-eminently *ho peirazon,* the tempter. It is thus that the Devil tempted Jesus in the wilderness (Matthew 4.1-11).

In this last sense *peirazein* is a bad word, for the action in it is designed to lure a man into sin.

(f) There is one last use of the word *peirazein* both in the Old and the New Testaments which is not strictly relevant for the purposes of our present investigation, but which for the sake of completeness we include. Frequently the Bible speaks of man tempting God (Exodus 17.2; Numbers 14.22; Isaiah 7.12; Matthew 4.7; Acts 15.10). The idea there is that a man tests God, in the sense of seeing how far he can go with God. He, as it were, tempts God to use his holy power; to put it in a colloquial phrase, he tries to see just how much he can get away with unpunished.

It can be seen that the word *peirasmos* is by no means easy to translate. It has in it three ideas. It has in it the simple idea of proving or testing the quality of a person or a thing. It has in it the idea of putting a person in a situation which is in reality a test but which involves the possibility of failure. And it has in it the idea of the deliberate invitation and seduction to sin. And the trouble about translating the word is that there is no one English word which does justice to the various ideas which reside in the word. The majority of the translations of this petition of the Lord's Prayer concentrate on the temptation side of the word. E. V. Rieu by using the word *ordeal,* and the NEB by using the word *test* concentrate almost entirely on the testing side of the word.

The English word which comes nearest to containing both ideas is the word *trial;* and it is significant to note that the RSV in at least eight instances substitutes the word *trial* for the AV *temptation* in the translation of the word *peirasmos.* So in Luke 22.28 Jesus speaks of the sharing of the disciples in his *trials.* Paul speaks to the

Ephesian elders of the *trials* which befell him (Acts
20.19). In James 1.2 the RSV substitutes *various trials*
for *divers temptations,* as it does in 1 Peter 1.6. Paul's
physical condition is a *trial* to the Galatians, not a
temptation (Galatians 4.14). The blessing is on the man
who endures *trials,* rather than temptations (James 1.12).
In 2 Peter 2.9 the RSV substitutes God knows "how
to rescue the godly from *trial*", for "how to deliver
the godly out of *temptation*". In Revelation 3.10 the
AV speaks of the hour of *temptation* which is coming on
the world; the RSV speaks about the hour of *trial;* and
the NEB of the *ordeal* that is to fall on the whole world.
And in all these passages the rendering is greatly im-
proved by the substitution of *trial* for *temptation.* A
peirasmos is an event or situation which tries a man.
It tries him in the sense that it is difficult to bear;
and it tries him in the sense that his reaction to it
shows what kind of a man he is.

From all this certain truths emerge in regard to the
Christian conception of temptation. We may say three
things about temptation.

i. Temptation is universal and inescapable, part and
parcel of the human situation. There is no man on
earth who does not need to pray this petition.

ii. Temptation is not outside the plan and the purpose of God. It is part of the structure of life and living
which God uses to make life what he meant it to be. The
ordeal of temptation is an integral factor in the making
of manhood.

iii. There is in temptation always an element of
probation. Temptation is always essentially a test. Even
when it is a seduction to sin, it is still a test of a man's
resistance power.

It thus becomes true to say that temptation is not so
much the penalty of manhood as it is the glory of man-

hood. It is that by which a man is made into the athlete of God.

iv. To this we may add the fourth fact. The very fact that we pray this petition is the proof that we are well aware that we cannot deal with temptation by ourselves, but that we need the power which is not our own in order that we may emerge triumphantly from the test.

When we remember this biblical view of temptation, it is clear that our problem is considerably simplified; it is not nearly so difficult to ascribe temptation, *peirasmos,* to the action of God; it is much easier to see how temptation can lie within the providence of God.

We may now go on to look at the two clauses of this petition in detail.

1. First, there is the clause, Lead us not into temptation. All that we have said about the word *peirasmos* is true, and the early Christian writers were perfectly well aware of the facts, and yet in spite of it all there remains in the word *peirasmos* an overtone of evil. Always at the back of it there is the idea that a *peirasmos* in any sense of the word is something which is calculated to, or at least liable to, take a man's faith and loyalty away. The interpretations of this clause have therefore in one way or another sought to avoid the implication that God would ever deliberately do anything to attack or injure any man's faith.

Sometimes an escape road has been found by attaching special meanings to different words in the clause.

i. A special stress has been laid upon the word *into.* *Into,* the Greek *eis,* could well stand for the Hebrew *lidhe,* which means *into the hands of,* and therefore *into the power of.* The meaning would then be something like this, if we put it into an amplified form: " I

know that temptation must come to me, for there can
be no life without temptation. But, when it does come,
as come it must, do not abandon me to it; do not
deliver me helpless into its power; stand by me in
my hour of need." This would not be very different
from Jesus' prayer for his disciples: " I do not pray
that thou shouldst take them out of the world, but
that thou shouldst keep them from the evil one "
(John 17.15). In that case this would not be so much
an impossible prayer to be exempted from temptation
as a prayer not to be abandoned helpless and unarmed
to its attack and to its power. To put it positively,
it would be a prayer for help when temptation comes.

ii. Augustine has an interpretation of this clause
much on the same lines. He draws a distinction (*The
Sermon on the Mount* 2.9) between *being tempted* and
being *brought into temptation*. All men must be
tempted; but to be brought into temptation is to be
brought into the power and the control of temptation;
it is to be not only subjected to temptation but to
be subdued by temptation.

Other writers have variations on this theme. In essence
this interpretation takes the clause to be a prayer not
for escape from temptation but for victory over temptation. Origen quotes the Greek version of Job 7.1
which says that all life is temptation, and then he goes
on: "Accordingly, let us pray to be delivered from
temptation, not that we should not be tempted—which
is impossible, especially for those on earth—but that we
may not yield when we are tempted . . . We should
pray then not that we may not be tempted—which is
impossible—but that we may not be brought under the
power of temptation, which happens to them who are
caught and captured by it " (*On Prayer* 29.9, 11).
Origen quotes the example of Job. Job, he says,
was delivered from temptation, not because the Devil

did not attack him; the Devil in point of fact launched every kind of attack upon him; but because no matter what befell him he did not sin before the Lord, and showed himself to be just (*On Prayer* 30.1, 2). The deliverance lay not in the exemption from temptation but in the conquest of it. Luther took the same view. "We cannot help," he said, "being exposed to the assaults, but we pray that we may not fall and perish under them."

Chrysostom goes even further. He takes the clause to mean, not only that we should not fall, but that we should not even enter into the struggle with temptation, lest we should fall. For him it is a prayer for the total elimination of temptation, but that is surely a prayer which cannot be answered within the human situation.

iii. There is still a third line of interpretation, and this line was very common in the early Church. Augustine says that there were actually manuscripts of the New Testament in Latin in his day which rendered this clause: "Do not allow us to be led into temptation." (*Ne nos induci patiaris in temptationem*). This is in fact the interpretation of Tertullian, Cyprian and Augustine (Augustine, *Sermon on the Mount* 2.9; *On the Gift of Perseverance* 6; Tertullian, *On Prayer* 8; Cyprian, *The Lord's Prayer* 25).

It may well be that this is the correct interpretation. The Syriac version of the New Testament renders this clause: "Do not *make us to enter into* temptations." The Hebrew verb has a large variety of forms and this would go back to the Hebrew form of the verb known as the *Hiph'il*. The *Hiph'il* is the causative form of the verb, and means to make a person do something or other. Now this *hiph'il* form of the verb can be *permissive* as well as *causative*, and it can mean to *allow* a person to do something or other, and if in the original of the prayer a *hiph'il* was used by Jesus, it will mean: "Do not allow us to enter into temptation", or: "Do not allow us to be led into temptation."

Here is an interpretation which gives us excellent sense, for in this case the meaning would be: " Keep us from flirting with temptation. Keep us from situations in which temptation will get its chance. Defend us from the assaults of temptation which come from our own nature and from the seductions of others. Defend us from the attacks of the world, the flesh and the devil." It would be a prayer that neither by our own weakness nor by the malice of others we may be brought into life situations in which we are foolishly and sometimes needlessly exposed to the attack of temptation. It would be a prayer in which we ask God to be the defender and the guardian of our faith, our loyalty and our purity.

These then are the main lines of interpretation of this clause, offered by those who hesitate to ascribe actual temptation to God, and certainly the last of them which turns the clause into a prayer for God's defending and preserving power is very attractive. But when all is said and done, there are two things to be said.

First, it is very doubtful if the Hebrew mind would have felt the difficulty of this clause. It is quite true that James says: " Let no man when he is tempted say, I am tempted by God " (James 1.13), but, when we read the whole of the James passage, and when we see what is really in James' mind, we see that James is really condemning the man who puts the blame for his own *sin* upon God. He is thinking of the man who holds God to be responsible for his sin. But the whole bent of the Hebrew mind was to think that everything, literally everything, is in the hands of God and under his control. Because of this the Hebrew mind would have found no difficulty in believing that even temptation somehow fits into the plan and the purpose of God. Looking back over life Joseph said of his brothers: "As for you, you meant evil against me; but God meant it for good" (Genesis 50.20). A Jew would not have found it difficult to believe that even apparent evil is woven into the pattern of God, since a Jew would have started out with the fundamental belief that nothing, literally nothing, can happen which is not the will of God.

Second, it may well be that in all our efforts at explanation we are allowing theological logic to take precedence over the natural human reaction of the heart.

To take a very simple human analogy and to put it in very simple and even colloquial terms, we can easily imagine a student saying to his teacher, or an athlete saying to his trainer, never doubting the love of the teacher or the good intent of the trainer: "Go easy with me! Don't push me too hard!" It may well be that this is the best way in which to approach this petition; it may be best simply to see in it the instinctive appeal of the man who knows how weak he is and how dangerous life can be, and who takes his own peril to the protection of God. For the theologian the theological problem may be there; for the human being the theological problem is lost in the instinctive appeal of the human need.

2. There is the clause, Deliver us from evil. As we have seen, the translations in this clause are divided between, Deliver us from evil, in the general sense of the term, and, Deliver us from the Evil One in the sense of the Devil, the personal power of evil. The Greek can equally well mean either, and in point of fact the variation in translation makes very little difference to the meaning.

It is well to understand what the biblical writers

understand by the Evil One. The Evil One goes under two names in the Bible.

(a) Sometimes he is called Satan. The word *satan* was not originally a proper name; it originally meant an *adversary* in the ordinary human sense of the term, and it is so used in Scripture seven times. The angel of the Lord is the adversary of Balaam, standing direct and opposing in his path (Numbers 22.22). Even when David appeared to throw in his lot with them, the Philistines fear that in battle he may turn out to be their adversary, their satan (1 Samuel 29.4). It is Solomon's thanksgiving that he has neither adversary (*satan*) nor misfortune (1 Kings 5.4). In later days both Hadad and Rezon are to become the *satans*, the adversaries, of Israel (1 Kings 11.14.23.25). A *satan* is simply an adversary.

Originally Satan was not an evil character; he was one of the sons of God (Job 1.6). But he had a special function. He was, so to speak, the prosecuting counsel against men; it was his function to say and to urge everything that could be said and urged against a man; he was man's adversary in the courts of God (Job 1.6-12). Satan is characteristically the Adversary of man.

(b) Sometimes he is called the Devil. In Greek the word Devil is *diabolos*. *Diabolos* was originally neither a proper name nor a title. It is the normal Greek word for *slanderer,* and it is so used in the New Testament. Women in the Church must be serious minded and not *slanderers* (1 Timothy 3.11). In the last days *slanderers* (false accusers, AV) will arise (2 Timothy 3.3). The older women are not to be *slanderers* (false accusers) or slaves to drink (Titus 2.3).

So then the word *Satan* describes the Adversary who is the prosecuting counsel against men; the word Devil, *diabolos,* describes the one who is *par excellence,* the slanderer. And the two ideas are not so very different, because it is not so very far a cry from stating the case against a man to fabricating a case against a man. The aim of the Evil One is by any means to cause a breach between man and God, to break the relationship between man and God. The Evil One is the personification of all that is against God and all that is out to ruin man in this life and in the life to come.

It makes little difference whether we speak of evil or of the Evil One. We know quite well that there is in this world a force of evil which attacks goodness and which invites to sin. That force may be a personal force, or that force may be what we might call the cumulative effect of all the evil acts and evil decisions which have been part of the human scene. Be the force personal or impersonal, it is there. And this prayer is the prayer that we may be armoured and protected against it, and that we may be strengthened in our resistance power to it.

" The Lord," we read in the second Letter to Timothy, "will rescue me from every evil, and save us for his heavenly kingdom" (2 Timothy 4.18). And Luther puts the matter at its widest: " In this prayer we ask our heavenly Father to set us free from all evil of body and soul, honour and estate: and finally, when our last hour comes, to vouchsafe us a happy end, and to take us from this valley of tears to himself in heaven." As Luther sees it, this is the prayer for rescue in life and rescue in death.

Lead us not into temptation, but deliver us from evil. This concluding petition of the Lord's Prayer does three things. First, it frankly faces the danger of the human situation. Second, it freely confesses the inadequacy of human resources to deal with it. Thirdly, it takes both the danger and the weakness to the protecting power of God. And when we do all this we can say with Cyprian (*The Lord's Prayer* 27): "When we have once asked for God's protection against evil and have obtained it, then against everything which the devil and the world can do against us, we stand secure and safe. For what fear is there in this life to the man whose Guardian in this life is God?"

EPILOGUE

The Lord's Prayer, as we commonly use it, has what we might call its own built-in epilogue, for it ends with the ascription of praise : " For thine is the kingdom and the power and the glory, for ever. Amen " (Matthew 6.13). As any of the newer translations will show this was not part of the original prayer and it is not in the earliest and the best manuscripts. Ultimately in the Church it became part of the prayer because it was the response of the congregation to the prayer. It is an ascription of praise with a very long history, for it goes right back to the prayer of David, when he was making the preparation for the Temple which his son Solomon was one day to build : " Thine, O Lord, is the greatness, and the power, and the glory, and the victory, and the majesty; for all that is in the heaven and the earth is thine; thine is the kingdom, O Lord, and thou art exalted as head above all " (1 Chronicles 29.11). So, then, almost since men first began to use the Lord's Prayer in public this has been the response of the worshipping people to it.

The great value of this conclusion to the Lord's Prayer is that it reminds us of two things. It reminds us to whom we have been praying, and it reminds us that, if prayer is to be complete we have to give as well as to take.

Thine is the kingdom. It may be that the word *kingdom* is misleading here. To us kingdom tends to mean an area of land within which a king's rule is exercised. So we would speak of the kingdom of Great Britain, meaning the country of Britain. But here in the Lord's Prayer the word does not so much mean *kingdom* as it means *kingship*. The kingship is God's; his is the royal power; it is his right to exercise the power and the authority of king. Simply to say to God : " Thine is the kingship; Thine is the royal power," should be in itself an act of submission to God. We end the prayer by recognising that God is king, that we are subjects, and by pledging our obedience and our allegiance to him.

Thine is the power. The word is *dunamis,* from which the English words *dynamic* and *dynamite* come. We end the prayer by reminding ourselves of the dynamic power of God. We end the prayer by thinking of the God in whom there is both the love to listen and the power to act. And, remembering that, we are bound to bring to God the trust and the confidence which his power demands. We end our prayer in the confidence that in his love God has heard, and that in his dynamic power he will answer.

Thine is the glory. The very word glory is a more than human word. We use the word loosely of the kind of honour and reputation and fame that some kind of human achievement can bring; but properly glory belongs to God alone. We end the prayer by reminding ourselves that we are in the presence of the divine glory; and that means that we must live life in the reverence which never forgets that it is living within the splendour of the glory of God.

And so, when we have prayed the Lord's Prayer, we rise from our knees and go out to the world and its ways remembering the royal sovereignty of God and pledged to obedience to him, remembering the dynamic power of God and trusting in that power to answer our prayers, remembering the glory of God and living with the reverence which knows that earth is penetrated and permeated with the divine glory.